Microsoft

Solutions

for

SUPPLIER

E_m_p_o_w_e_r_m_e_n_t>

Business-to-Business

E-Commerce

Martin Harwar
Andy Longshaw
Robert Hylton

PUBLISHED BY
Microsoft Press
A Division of Microsoft Corporation
One Microsoft Way
Redmond, Washington 98052-6399

Copyright © 2002 by Microsoft Corporation

Library of Congress Cataloging-in-Publication Data
Harwar, Martin.
    Supplier Empowerment / Martin Harwar, Andy Longshaw, Robert Hylton.
      p. cm.
    Includes index.
    ISBN 0-7356-1498-9
    1. Electronic commerce. 2. Industrial marketing. I. Longshaw, Andy. II. Hylton,
Robert. III. Title.

HF5548.32 .H3726   2002
658.8'4--dc21   2001058732

Printed and bound in the United States of America.

1 2 3 4 5 6 7 8 9   QWT   7 6 5 4 3 2

Distributed in Canada by Penguin Books Canada Limited.

A CIP catalogue record for this book is available from the British Library.

Microsoft Press books are available through booksellers and distributors worldwide. For further
information about international editions, contact your local Microsoft Corporation office or
contact Microsoft Press International directly at fax (425) 936-7329. Visit our Web site at
www.microsoft.com/mspress. Send comments to *mspinput@microsoft.com*.

bCentral, BizTalk, Microsoft, Microsoft Press, MSN, SharePoint, and Windows are either
registered trademarks or trademarks of Microsoft Corporation in the United States and/or
other countries. Other product and company names mentioned herein may be the trademarks of their respective owners.

The example companies, organizations, products, domain names, e-mail addresses, logos, people,
places, and events depicted herein are fictitious. No association with any real company, organization, product, domain name, e-mail address, logo, person, place, or event is intended or should be
inferred.

Acquisitions Editor: Alex Blanton
Project Editor: Kristen Weatherby

Body Part No. X08-63861

Contents

Preface

For almost three years, the business-to-business electronic commerce software industry has been covered from nearly every angle and through every medium. From supply chain to marketplaces, from procurement to design collaboration, and so on, the sheer amount of coverage is bewildering. So why create another book on the subject? Put simply, the role of the single largest and arguably the most significant group of participants in business-to-business trade, the suppliers, has seen little coverage to date, and over the past several years research and industry changes have shed new light on the dramatic benefits that suppliers can achieve by automating how they sell to business customers.

While many of these changes have included advances in technology, this book has been written primarily for businesspeople. Key to our target audience is chief executive officers, sales and marketing executives, information technology executives, and operations executives. While we think there is also value for technical audiences, the primary objective is to introduce and expose the business benefits of leveraging technology and to provide guidance for increasing the chances of overall success. Obviously, the business objectives of any effort should be understood by everyone involved.

This book has clearly been a team effort. With our combined efforts and industry experience, we—Martin Harwar, Robert Hylton, and Andy Longshaw—and the entire team at Microsoft Press worked tirelessly to expose many years of knowledge and research in a form that will provide insight, guidance, and possibly some clarity to a topic often referred to as "chaos." Additionally, the actual suppliers that adopted the strategies and technology solutions and allowed us to tell their stories, along with the partners that implemented them, deserve even more credit. Without real examples of success (and struggles), the business concepts and the technology solutions presented here wouldn't be worth much more than the paper they are printed on. Literally hundreds of individuals and companies, from as nearby as Redmond (Washington) to as far away as Route de lu Borde (France) contributed to the concepts and strategies contained in this book.

The objective of this book is not to sell a particular product or solution per se. However, Microsoft's approach and solutions for achieving benefits and solving business issues are presented as examples throughout because they have been created specifically to satisfy the demands of suppliers engaging in business-to-business trade, as outlined in the following chapters.

We sincerely hope that our efforts and our point of view provide value and insight to your future endeavors and have a positive impact on your overall success, regardless of the role you play. To that point, we welcome any feedback about the book or your own efforts. Please feel free to contact us at *mssebook@hotmail.com.*

Introduction

The combination of today's business and technology environments offers companies of all sizes dynamic and exciting business opportunities, but it is rife with uncertainties and challenges. Although most analysts still expect the volume of goods and services sold between businesses via the Internet to climb into the trillions of dollars worldwide in the next few years, the uncertainty has by no means decreased. In the face of all the confusion surrounding business-to-business (B2B) e-commerce, most companies are struggling to understand where their real opportunities lie and how they can make strategic technology investments that align with today's business objectives while providing the flexibility to help them respond to rapid changes in the business landscape.

To uncover some of these mysteries, it is important to understand the history that created such fascinating opportunities and the chaos that followed.

What a Ride!

In early 1999, the word *e-commerce* was just starting to mean something to businesses outside the technology industry. Online retailers, such as Amazon.com, Barnes & Noble, and others, had just seen their first major holiday rush along with new levels of frustration behind the pretty Web sites viewed by consumers. The ability to reach customers 24 hours a day, 7 days a week, the fact that e-commerce had finally reached mainstream (and at high volume), and the emergence of business issues such as fulfillment and demand forecasting all started to ring in the ears of those that focused on trading between businesses. In addition, there were a new breed of technology vendors and solution providers emerging to take advantage of these new trends. This was merely the beginning of what would be an amazing two years for everyone involved.

The term business-to-business e-commerce, or B2B e-commerce, became mainstream in 1999 around several main scenarios, most of which were not new business problems but ones that changed dramatically with advances in technology, specifically the Internet. These scenarios included supply-chain management (demand planning, demand forecasting, inventory replenishment, logistics, etc.), procurement, travel and expense management, design collaboration, electronic marketplaces, and many others. Again, most companies had some solutions to these issues in place, but the technology used to solve them was about to change rapidly, as was the hype surrounding it.

The B2B Hype Meter

So what really created the dramatic acceleration of B2B e-commerce that year? The answer can be found by looking at the previous trend for large organizations: enterprise resource planning (ERP). ERP applications, such as SAP and Oracle, had seen amazing growth in the mid-1990s and had been implemented by most of the Fortune 1000 companies at amazing levels of investment and with significant amounts of organizational change. These applications were very sophisticated, took a long time to sell and even longer to implement, and, most importantly, did not have a single, quantifiable value proposition for the customer; rather, they had many propositions that cut across multiple parts of an organization and affected many individuals. In the late 1990s, companies were looking for a return from these massive investments, but even though it was there, it was difficult to see. Electronic procurement changed the rules on this.

Put simply, electronic procurement was an application that could show dramatic return on the investment (and the ERP systems already in place), was easy to explain (to customers, press, analysts, and investors), and was already proven by many customers. Microsoft, for example, built its own Web-based procurement application in 1995 and has been saving millions per year with relatively little effort. Microsoft's e-procurement implementation is one of many case studies that brought this scenario to the forefront in the industry as the next big technology wave for businesses. Also, electronic procurement software vendors, such as Ariba and Commerce One, went public in 1995 and saw amazing gains on the stock market—the acceleration had begun.

Once these new vendors, along with others in the market, such as Clarus, i2 Technologies, SAP, and Oracle, became recognized for this new breed of application and its use of the Internet, a race had begun to see which company could out maneuver the others with its business strategy, its technology, and its ability to create awareness among customers and investors (the latter was often the primary focus). This "race for hype" created the next big wave in B2B: the electronic marketplace. Marketplaces (stock markets, commodity markets, etc.) were not a new concept to the average businessperson, but this new breed promised results for the vendors and customers that were unimaginable just 12 months earlier. At one point, one technology vendor was valued on the stock market at over US $40 billion dollars, had about 200 customers, and was losing money. By comparison, this company had become over 1/10th the value of Microsoft, which had somewhere in the neighborhood of 300 million customers and significant profits.

This created the first problem: these new strategies, the associated public relations wave, and the stock market value of these technology vendors moved at a pace with which actual technology and customers were not prepared to keep up. The hype had outpaced any software company's ability to produce high-quality enterprise applications that fulfilled these amazing promises. It became the industry's problem as a whole, and customers were left to find the reality hidden amongst the chaos. The good news was that the reality wasn't that bad, but, like the dot-com failures of the year before, it was about to be shaken up.

The B2B software industry started seeing hard times at the end of 2000 for several reasons. The first has already been mentioned: the market hype had outgrown the vendor's ability to keep up. The applications, specifically marketplaces, were very new applications in a very immature market, and the customers, many of which were new companies (market makers), were just as immature. The press started printing articles about low volumes of trade through marketplaces, along with stories of errors, poor customer service, and the beginning of B2B marketplace closures. Secondly, many of the same technology vendors had grown at such a rapid pace and entered so many new markets (supply chain management, logistics, manufacturing, etc.) that they lost much of their focus on the core problem they had begun to solve: efficient procurement. These two reasons were important, but it was the third that took the most significant toll on the vendors and the industry as a whole: supplier enablement.

Both electronic procurement and marketplace applications rely on significant transaction volume in order to provide ROI to the companies that invest in the technology. For example, Microsoft processes over 500,000 transactions per year through its procurement system. The higher the transaction volume is, the higher the savings will be. For marketplaces, the higher the transaction volume is, the more the transaction fees and revenue will be. This concept of market liquidity is not new; however, a key participant to achieving success had been amazingly left out. The buyers and market makers had been catered to significantly, but where were the suppliers? To the surprise of many, large quantities of suppliers didn't show up to the party, even after some of their largest customers did. The reason? They were presented with little or no value for their participation, and, in many cases, it threatened their business. The value was (and is) there, but it required a deeper appreciation for suppliers' business and what makes it successful.

Light at the End of the Tunnel?

The good news is that electronic trade has a significant future, as long as there is value to *all* of the participants. Patience and awareness are paramount to achieving the promised benefits, and those that treat technology as a strategic weapon, as opposed to a cost of doing business, will no doubt reap the rewards. Although the following chapters concentrate on the role of the supplier in business-to-business trade, it is important to grasp just how dramatic the impact of the Internet, other new advances in technology, and emerging business models will be for everyone involved.

The Role of Suppliers in Business-to-Business E-Commerce

Trading is essential to our survival as a species! We know that Charles Darwin had no need to consider such a statement when he was studying wildlife on the Galapagos Islands (but how *did* he think that his ship, *The Beagle,* materialized?). He had other things on his mind, so we'll leave it at that. (Also, the editorial team is expecting a book about suppliers, not the origin of species, and we don't want to alienate them, especially this early in the book.)

Throughout history, and even in prehistoric times, people have traded with each other. Trading existed even before we invented money as a standard way to apply value to goods and, later, services. Trade links now spread from your hometown all the way across the world, which is probably why you picked up this book. (If there are reasons other than the fact that you are interested in improving the way you do business today and in the future, we'd really like to know. You can find details about how to contact us inside the back cover.)

Throughout human history, there have been some notable step changes in trading practices. The Agricultural Revolution gave rise to the organized exchange of goods. The Industrial Revolution brought the manufacturing of products to the forefront and introduced requirements for ancillary services. Such services have, in recent times, gone on to eclipse those very manufacturing activities. (On this time scale, anything in the last few decades is "recent.") In *very* recent times (the last few years), information has become one of the most valuable and most traded commodities. In fact, we are often told that we are living in the Information Age and that the Information Revolution has occurred.

The Agricultural Revolution demanded a new infrastructure to support the exchange of goods, such as new trade routes, corn exchanges, and market towns. The Industrial Revolution introduced its own infrastructure changes, including canals, railways, ships, shipping channels, and factories. The Information Revolution has also brought with it a new infrastructure. You will have heard of this infrastructure—it is called the Internet.

Each revolution in business practices has brought an increase in the reach that traders can achieve. The Agricultural Revolution allowed trade on a regional scale. The Industrial Revolution saw this trade extended to the scale of empires. The advent of the Internet has completed this expansion by allowing trade between all companies, no matter where they are physically located. The speed and efficiency with which goods, services, and information are traded has also increased, along with the reach of trading partners, with each step change. During the Industrial Revolution, canals, steamships, and railways replaced horses and carts. Now the Internet is used to exchange business data, far outstripping the speed and capacity of postal services.

Because both the Internet and the way in which it is used to trade goods, services, and information are still evolving, we are still in the middle of this revolution. The Internet offers important opportunities to improve the way in which we conduct business. New business models are emerging from these opportunities at a phenomenal rate, and some of them disappear just as quickly. Headline writers often build up one business model or another as a visionary example of opportunity, only to castigate the proponents of those ideas when flaws are revealed.

You need think only of the rapid demise of some companies in the wake of the dot-com frenzy that surrounded the turn of the millennium to realize that the Internet alone is not a panacea for all business strategies. Some of the business models proposed for this new environment failed to take into account all of the underlying principles of trading and, with hindsight, were only really sustained by the newness of the infrastructure. However, even though many business initiatives are flawed, they are nevertheless important to the evolution of new, better ideas. We all learn by experience.

We think of the Internet much as the leaders of the Industrial Revolution may have viewed the canals or railways: the use of the infrastructure is not the be all and the end all. During the Industrial Revolution, many ideas must have emerged about how canals could be used for new business purposes. The better ideas would have evolved along with the canal network, whereas flawed schemes would have disappeared.

In the United Kingdom, there is a well-known phrase that is often used to describe ideas not supported by business logic: "That's like sending coal to Newcastle!" (Newcastle was a major coal-producing and exporting area of the United Kingdom during the Industrial Revolution, so the last thing people there needed was *more* coal.) Because most coal was transported by canal at the time, this saying captures the idea that a perfectly good infrastructure could be used for business initiatives that might be foolhardy. As with canals, so with the Internet—the aim should always be to create a good business strategy that uses the infrastructure to its best advantage.

Throughout this book, we will discuss many issues and concepts that relate to online trading, using the Internet as the infrastructure. We will examine new business models that have evolved along with the Internet. We will identify well-founded ideas and provide cautionary advice that has been learned from recent initiatives. As this volume is targeted at empowering suppliers so that they can participate in this business revolution, we will focus specifically on issues that affect how organizations can benefit from making their goods and services available using the Internet. That is not to say we will completely ignore the perspective of their customers, or buyer organizations—in fact, most companies are both suppliers *and* buyers. Further, the many and varied ways in which suppliers interact with buyers is one of the key areas of discussion in this book.

In this chapter, we provide some scene-setting and background information. You may have already gained experience in the field of business-to-business (B2B) e-commerce, but we advise you to at least skim through this introductory material because it provides the basis for some ideas that we expand on later in the book. Also, this chapter firmly sets the scene from the perspective of supplier organizations.

Introduction to B2B E-Commerce

B2B e-commerce involves the trading of goods and services between businesses using the Internet. More specifically, B2B e-commerce is concerned with using the infrastructure of the Internet as a basis for the *communication* involved in the buying and selling process. A substantial amount of information is typically involved in a business transaction, and you must not lose sight of the fact that this information is exchanged ultimately to support a very simple concept—the exchange of goods or services for money (or other value). Such information includes purchase orders, invoices, and receipts, among other things. Traditionally, the majority of this data has been paper-based.

Given the advent of the Information Revolution, data is generated and consumed by businesses at a phenomenal rate. Using paper-based systems to exchange this amount of data is fast becoming unfeasible, and it is certainly inefficient. It is a challenge to keep track of all this data, and it is increasingly difficult to manage just the volume of information, let alone to use it constructively to improve the way business is done. The need to both represent and exchange business data electronically has long been obvious.

Some organizations have been exchanging business data electronically for decades and benefiting from this type of exchange. They have been able to exchange, manage, and analyze vast amounts of data effectively, simply because it is in some type of electronic format. This general approach has long been viewed as desirable to many businesses. You may find it surprising, then, that the vast majority of commercial organizations did not follow suit years ago. Briefly, the reasons for this are that many of the first systems that allowed business data to be exchanged electronically were expensive and difficult to implement. Such systems, known as electronic data interchange (EDI) systems, are also proprietary in nature. Only the largest corporations could afford to commission and implement such systems, and even then they were faced with integration and customization difficulties.

The emergence of the Internet as a cheaper, faster, more flexible mechanism for exchanging business data electronically has reintroduced the possibility that businesses of all sizes and capacities can exchange data this way. The Internet itself is not a complete solution to the problem, however. Many issues about the electronic exchange of information still persist, such as evolving standards for representing, delivering, and manipulating data. This is to be expected, because we are in the middle of the Information Revolution, and the Internet itself is still evolving.

Since the late 1990s, interest in B2B e-commerce has been intense. This interest has arisen from a concept that is familiar to us all—making money. A key part of this is simply the huge potential that business can see for reducing costs by automating and streamlining business processes. The Internet can be used as a cheap and flexible infrastructure to achieve these goals for online trading. Another incentive is the huge volume of trade that is predicted for B2B e-commerce. The Gartner Group predicted in early 2001 that B2B revenues would climb to $7.29 trillion by the year 2004. Gartner went on to surmise that, at that time, B2B e-commerce transactions would also represent 7 percent of the $105 trillion total sales worldwide. These predictions had providers of B2B services licking their lips in anticipation of capturing even a small fraction of that money.

An overall goal for B2B e-commerce is to allow companies, whether they are suppliers or buyers, to streamline their interactions with trading partners. However, the number of different visions and ideas that have emerged around B2B e-commerce make it easy to perceive the whole issue as chaotic. When we consider the requirements of electronic trading, the fact that buyers have so many different ways to interact with suppliers muddies the water still further. Add to this the emergence of companies seeking to provide services for the process of online trading, each with their own perspective and objectives, and the overall issue can appear bewildering.

Over the next few pages, we will clarify the different roles involved in B2B e-commerce. We will then move on to discuss recent trends and business models, and then conclude this chapter with a discussion of the challenges and opportunities facing suppliers in today's business environment.

B2B E-Commerce Roles

You are certainly familiar with some of the roles involved in B2B e-commerce. For example, everyone knows what a buyer is, in general terms, and could also provide definitions for a supplier. Other roles, such as market makers or Web service providers, may not be as familiar. Our goal for this section of the chapter is to provide clarification of the different roles that have an interest in B2B e-commerce and to briefly outline their positions.

Suppliers

You may have guessed from the title of this book that we are looking at the B2B e-commerce landscape from the perspective of suppliers. The issues affecting suppliers are many and varied—the bulk of this book addresses those issues, including the aims of suppliers, the challenges they face in achieving those goals, and strategies for overcoming those challenges. Because it is not possible to do justice to all of these topics in a few short paragraphs, we restrict this section to a brief discussion of the supplier focus—the rest of this book will delve into all of those other issues.

Most commercial organizations not only purchase goods and services from other companies, but also sell goods or services to other businesses. Almost all companies are both buyers and suppliers. Whereas the procurement, or buy-side, of a business is primarily concerned with using the Internet for efficiency gains in how business purchases are made, the supply-side of a business has major goals of reducing costs and increasing revenue by using the Internet to sell goods or services. We will delve into these and other supplier objectives in *Chapter 2, "Business-to-Business E-Commerce Objectives for Suppliers."*

Buyers

As you might expect, any company that purchases goods or services from another organization is a buyer. As already stated, most companies are both buyers and suppliers to some degree. However, some businesses definitely have a distinct emphasis on buying, as far as their interest in B2B e-commerce is concerned. Consider a large aircraft manufacturer—it is certainly in business to supply airplanes and helicopters to its customers. However, those customers are likely to be few in number, compared to the suppliers that the company uses on a daily basis. The manufacturer might well have tens of airlines and governments placing orders for its aircraft, but it will have tens of thousands, if not hundreds of thousands, of suppliers that provide the company with everything from steel, nuts and bolts, and plastics, to stationery, office equipment, computers, coffee, and professional services. Such a company might not deem the ability for its customers to order the latest passenger jet over the Internet a dramatic improvement over current practices. It will, however, clearly see the benefits of ordering coffee, steel, or office chairs in a more streamlined, efficient manner.

Benefits of Automated Procurement to Buyer Organizations

The ability to place orders with suppliers in an automated manner is one of the most attractive benefits of B2B e-commerce for buyers. In one scenario, automated procurement may involve an employee at a buyer organization placing a business order with a supplier using a simple Web browser. At the other end of the scale, an "intelligent" application may detect low stocks and automatically place orders, subject to business rules that are defined by the purchasing company. For the purpose of this section, we do not differentiate between the different types of automated procurement scenarios—we will deal with that later in the book.

The most obvious reason for automating the procurement process can be summed up in a single word: efficiency. Now, efficiency is rarely sought for its own sake—it is the reduction in cost for a given process that makes efficiency a sought-after goal. Automated procurement solutions provide a reduction in the transaction cost of making a purchase simply by introducing efficiency gains in that process. Most of the cost is incurred by using employee time to process the purchase. For example, employees may need to complete paper-based orders, send those orders to the suppliers, process and settle the resulting invoices, manage receipts, and so on. The industry-average cost for manually processing the data associated with a purchase is well over $100 (in the United States). It is only too common for an employee to decide that he or she needs a new stapler, costing, let's say, $3, but for the company to incur a cost for that purchase of many times the price of the product. The goal for buyers, then, is to reduce the costs incurred in the procurement process by making the process more efficient.

At Microsoft, we have a home-grown example of the savings that can be gained from increased efficiency by using an automated procurement application. Microsoft employees use an intranet tool called MS Market to place orders for various goods and services, such as stationery, computers, marketing materials, catering supplies, and so on. Microsoft uses more than 23,000 suppliers to service these requirements. With those suppliers, Microsoft carries out over a half-million individual transactions per year. Before MS Market, the average cost per transaction was about $65, so Microsoft was already operating at well below the industry average. Using MS Market, the cost is now between $5 and $10 per transaction. So, for each of those half-million transactions that Microsoft carries out each year, the savings to the company amount to $55 to $60. In other words, the savings amount to almost $30 million per year. This is especially remarkable given that we would not even classify Microsoft as a particularly purchasing-oriented company. It has limited need for raw materials and very few components or parts to purchase. The bulk of their purchases are made for maintenance, repair, and operations (MRO), such as office supplies, computers, and services.

Although we are not dismissing $30 million of savings as insignificant, there are certainly companies that spend a lot more than Microsoft and purchase a much wider range of goods and services. Savings for these companies can no doubt amount to significantly higher figures. Think back to our large manufacturer of aircraft—it would probably buy more office supplies than Microsoft *and* purchase huge amounts of steel, aluminum, plastics, rubber, and so on.

Although the figures we have described overwhelmingly support the case for many buyers to automate their procurement process (which is why we included them), they do not provide the whole story. For many organizations, including Microsoft, there is an even more important benefit of streamlining the procurement process. This benefit derives not from the decrease in transaction costs, but from the increased efficiency that such an application delivers for *all* employees. There are more than 50,000 people working at Microsoft at any given time (including contractors) who have access to MS Market. Those workers are located in more than 60 different countries. It is important to understand the nature of these people's employment: Microsoft is largely a knowledge-based company, and the workers are paid to use their brains (and time) efficiently. The automated procurement features of MS Market allow a significant saving of time in day-to-day tasks, such as booking travel or keeping office supply stocks at an appropriate level. Imagine that MS Market saves each employee even just *one* hour per year—that equates to 50,000 hours that can be used more productively each year. Assuming an eight-hour day, that's 6250 workdays (or 25 employee-years) of productivity gain.

This should give you some insight into the motivation behind many buyers' moves toward B2B e-commerce. In addition to cost and efficiency savings, other benefits can be achieved by automating procurement and related processes. These include the ability to apply business intelligence techniques to the data collected from automated systems, and the use of such systems to build strategic relationships with suppliers. We will not put a dollar figure against these other advantages because the mathematics involved in assessing the return from enhanced business relationships can get tricky! Also, bear in mind that the figures we have given are rough estimates and apply only to our Microsoft example.

Market Makers

Market makers are not a new element of the economy in general, but they only began emerging in the B2B e-commerce arena toward the end of the 1990s. The characteristics that define a market maker are many and varied—it is difficult to find two such companies that are alike. Some of these differences stem from the fact that many new business models, which generally fit under this banner, have sprung up and evolved rapidly over the last couple of years. Many of these models have also disappeared at a rapid rate. What we will do to clarify this matter is outline a brief history of this special type of company to give you an idea of what they are all about. Later in the chapter we will look at the role that market makers will play in the future.

Market makers emerged in B2B commerce with the goal of improving the efficiency of trade in a particular segment, such as a vertical industry or a particular company's supply chain. Market makers created marketplaces that, for a fee, connected buyers and sellers with each other. This took the burden and effort of making these connections away from the buyers, and the fees were often charged to the suppliers.

The perspective of a buyer organization in such a situation is clear: automating the procurement process can save a significant amount of money by introducing efficiency gains. The perspective of suppliers, as far as such solutions go, is not clear at all. For instance, out of Microsoft's 23,000 suppliers, only a small percentage actually integrated with MS Market originally to allow fully automated trading. Although these suppliers are among some of the companies with which Microsoft exercises a significant proportion of its spending, it leaves far too many suppliers out of the equation. The reason for this extremely low adoption rate by suppliers (and this rate is not atypical) is that although the use of automated procurement systems appears to be clean and efficient from inside the buyer organization, the same is not true for the supplier. Such procurement solutions were based on direct connections (known as *point-to-point* connections) between buyers and suppliers, which are expensive. Establishing and maintaining such connections, not just for one buyer, but for all of them, could amount to a significant cost for a supplier. The benefits to the supplier of such an arrangement were not well defined at that point. Without a substantive value proposition for integrating with thousands of different buyers and their procurement systems, the cost associated with hooking up to multiple buyers made the choice an easy one for many chief financial officers (CFOs) at supplier companies.

Figure 1-1 shows just how complicated life could become for suppliers if they had to maintain connections with, and consolidate data from, multiple business customers.

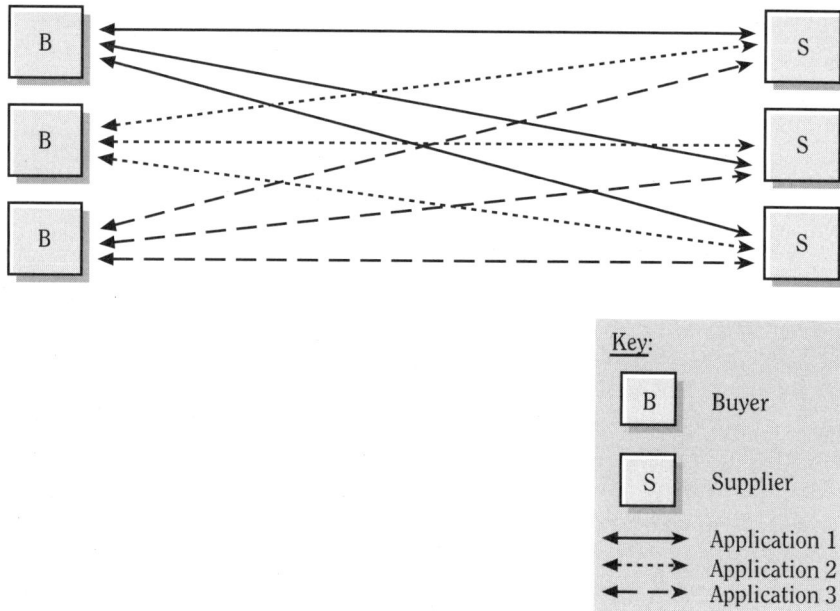

Figure 1-1. *Buyers see the impact of only one type of procurement application. Ideally, from their point of view, all of their suppliers would integrate with their solution to trade electronically. Suppliers, however, see multiple connections to multiple purchasing applications—potentially unique for each of their customers. This makes running their business extremely complicated.*

You might be asking yourself what all this has to do with market makers. Well, the very first Internet-based market makers decided that there was a central problem with the sort of solution described so far, namely that there were many of these buyers and suppliers and that they had significant gains to be had from electronic trade, but limited know-how or ability to take advantage of this new medium.

As we have discussed already, having to make multiple connections to multiple trading partners is a major drawback for all organizations. Market makers evangelized that the Internet could be used so that both suppliers *and* buyers need make only one connection, regardless of how many trading partners they needed to deal with. This idea quickly evolved to the stage where various market makers were proposing a *hub-and-spoke* model for allowing multiple buyers and multiple suppliers to trade electronically. Figure 1-2 shows a typical hub-and-spoke model.

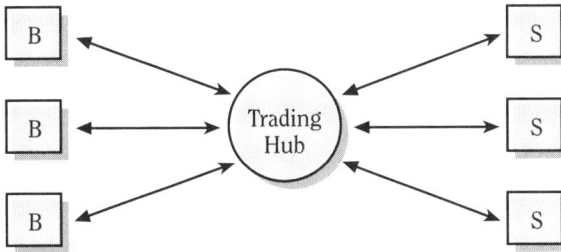

Figure 1-2. *A hub-and-spoke theoretical model for online trading. Each supplier and each buyer need only make one connection to the Internet to communicate with many trading partners.*

Now, market makers were not just proposing this sort of model for philanthropic reasons. They, like suppliers and buyers, are in business to make money. The primary basis for generating revenue, then, was that they would charge for routing business data through their hubs. For example, they would route messages over the Internet in a standard format (based on Extensible Markup Language [XML]), which would allow them to deal with the exchange of business data between supplier and buyer. Such data would include product information and catalogs, purchase orders, shipping details, invoices, receipts, and so on. Fees would be charged for this basic functionality, most often to suppliers.

On top of that, they saw plenty of opportunities for adding value to whatever went on in their hubs. Such ways to make money from controlling hubs included the provision of value-added services that buyers and suppliers might need as their messages flow through the hub. One example is the provision of consolidated payment services, in which the market maker can interact with banks and clearing houses to manage the monetary settlement of all transactions for buyers and sellers. Other examples of value-added services include advertising, managing online auctions, allowing shipping status to be checked for particular purchase orders, and many others.

The activities of the market makers resulted in a type of hub-and-spoke solution called an *electronic marketplace* or *electronic trading exchange*. As with the characteristics of the market makers themselves, no two marketplaces look alike. Each has its own identifying features and all function within different business models to varying degrees.

Marketplaces have emerged in all sorts of business areas since their inception. There are online marketplaces for trading everything from cattle to steel. The aerospace industry uses them, as does the oil and gas sector. In addition, marketplaces have not been restricted to vertical industry sectors, such as those already mentioned—there are also regional, horizontally aligned marketplaces. For example, a regional marketplace exists for general trading among Latin American companies. Even more significant, as time passes and business models become more realistic, is the creation of private marketplaces, or those exchanges run by the large organizations for trading within their community of suppliers and customers.

Hopefully, we have given you at least a point of reference for what a market maker is, in B2B e-commerce terms, and also what constitutes a marketplace or exchange. We will return to market makers and marketplaces when we discuss recent trends in B2B e-commerce. We will also outline where we think marketplaces are going in the near-to-mid-term. For now, bear in mind that not all marketplace-type initiatives have been successful. Strange and wonderful business models were proposed, some of which have had reasonable success, and many others that have faded into obscurity.

Web Service Providers

Just as market makers emerged to service the needs of buyers and suppliers that needed to trade using the Internet, another type of company has evolved to provide business services in this same arena. Such companies are typically called *Web service providers,* which is a fairly descriptive name. Just for clarification, this type of company provides *business* services, using the Internet as the infrastructure.

Note   At this point, we should make clear the distinction between *Web service providers and Internet service providers* (ISPs). They have similar names, but very different roles. ISPs supply the physical infrastructure that allows anyone from the largest corporation down to the smallest household to *connect* to the Internet. Web service providers, on the other hand, do not typically provide the infrastructure itself—rather, they provide business services that can be accessed over the Internet. We provide some examples of Web services in the sidebar.

Examples of Web Services

The following list provides some examples of Web services that are commonly used in B2B e-commerce:

- Payment
- Credit/financing
- Currency conversion
- Logistics
- Product design
- Authentication
- Language conversion
- Insurance
- Notification
- Escrow
- Shipping
- Classification
- Taxation
- Import/export
- Vendor rating
- Auctioning
- Calendaring

This list is not exhaustive—the provision of Web services is an emerging industry, and new ones are constantly being designed and developed. We provide some descriptions of some Web services and compare them to traditional business services in the main body of the text.

Web service providers offer a wide range of facilities that can be used over the Internet. The services that they offer bear comparison with facilities available to businesses trading in the traditional world. Imagine that you run a small construction company. The aspects of the business with which you are most familiar include the actual building process, the purchasing of materials, the provision of quotes and estimates to your customers, and so on. If you need to draw up contracts with customers, it is likely that you will hire the services of a law firm. If you need to prepare annual tax returns, you might use an accountancy firm. Instead of familiarizing yourself with modern computing techniques, you might outsource many of your information technology (IT) requirements to experts in that field.

Doing all of this has a number of advantages for your company. One such advantage is that your valuable time can be used to actually run your company, which is in the building trade, not the legal, accounting, or IT profession. This is, after all, why you are in business. Another advantage is that lawyers, accountants, and IT professionals have all spent many years becoming experts in their respective fields. You could not hope to achieve the same level of competence in all of these areas in a time frame that your company can afford. Yet another advantage is that you need only pay for the services provided by these experts when you need them. On top of all this, the companies that provide specialized services can more easily keep up with new developments in their particular fields—the accountancy firm will no doubt be aware of changes in tax legislation, the IT specialists will be aware of technology advances, and the lawyers will be up-to-date with matters affecting company law. All in all, it makes sense to use these services in most circumstances. In turn, you might expect a call from the law firm when it needs a new partition to be built in its offices!

As far as using the specialized services of other companies is concerned, conducting business electronically shares some similarities with the traditional approach to running a company. Just as our fictitious construction company could make good use of legal, accounting, and IT services, online traders can make use of specialized services available for B2B e-commerce. The nature of these services is varied. Some provide functionality that can be directly compared to traditional business services. For example, credit-card authentication services are required both for paper-based and Web-based business processes. The same is true for other Web-based financial services such as currency conversion, payment clearing, and money transfers.

Other Web-based services might have characteristics that do not easily afford comparisons with traditional business services—they might well have emerged as a response to the new requirements of B2B e-commerce. Examples of this type of service include calendaring and scheduling facilities. Of course, your company will probably have managed schedules before, but companies that provide such Web services have simply identified a need: businesses now demand complex scheduling functionality incorporated into their B2B processes and shared among trading partners, but they may be unable (or unwilling) to implement this functionality themselves. In short, they need the services of a company that specializes in the provision of shared online scheduling functionality. In fact, that is the crux of the issue—Web service providers are there to make functionality that falls into their area of expertise available to the wider B2B community, just as lawyers and accountants have done for centuries in the traditional business environment. A decision about whether you use a particular service, such as currency conversion or calendaring, should be viewed on a similar basis as to whether you use the services of an accounting company.

Before we get too carried away with drawing analogies between accounting firms and Web-based services, we should point out one thing: whereas traditional business services are essentially provided to human beings, Web services are provided to computer applications. These services are requested and delivered electronically, so whereas you pick up the phone or arrange a meeting to talk to your accountant, your e-commerce solution interacts with Web-based services over the Internet.

We hope you now have at least a point of reference for the role a Web service provider plays in B2B e-commerce. We will continue to discuss Web service providers and how they have interacted with market makers. We will then take an overall look at the roles each can play as B2B e-commerce continues to evolve.

Recent Trends and New Business Models

Over the past few years, the concept of using the Internet as a cheap, ubiquitous infrastructure for trading online has seeded many exciting new ideas. Those ideas have crystallized and brought about new companies, such as Web service providers and market makers, that can fulfill certain requirements for B2B e-commerce between buyers and suppliers. To describe how these different companies interact today and to lay the groundwork for how they will interact in the future, we briefly recap the recent history in this area.

Why Won't You Sell to Me?

The year 1999 saw a lot of attention being lavished on automated procurement systems. Theoretically (and even in practice from time to time), large buying organizations could realize significant savings by streamlining their procurement processes. Savings in the order of millions of dollars per year (and more) were being talked about, and in some cases, realized.

You can imagine the sort of media and stock market attention these systems were attracting. As discussed already, one big problem with the approach was the extremely low adoption rate of suppliers. Understandably, buyer organizations were tremendously keen to gain the participation of their suppliers in the automated procurement processes; otherwise, the anticipated benefits would not be realized. In fact, unless a certain number of suppliers were willing to participate, it would be a waste of the buyer's time and money to implement such systems. It is certainly not unheard of for a buyer to indicate to its suppliers that they would lose that company's business unless they integrated with a particular procurement system in place at the buyer's organization. In many cases, this incentive was still not enough for the CFO at the supplier organization. Figure 1-3 illustrates the buyer-centric nature of automated procurement until 1999.

Buyer-Centric Automated Procurement

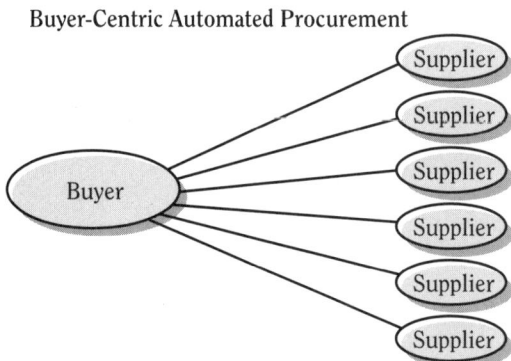

Figure 1-3.   *Buyer-centric procurement systems appeared to have a poor value proposition to suppliers. Expensive connections were only part of the problem. Other issues, such as integrating with many different proprietary systems for many different customers and the ability to differentiate, proved to be major drawbacks for suppliers.*

Eventually, people realized just how prohibitive to supplier participation the costs and risks associated with such systems were.

We've Invented the Wheel!

Something had to be done, and quickly! Enter the market maker around the turn of the millennium. As we discussed earlier, market makers proposed a hub-and-spoke model for connecting suppliers and buyers. To put things into context, the market makers typically evolved from those that had offered solutions for earlier automated procurement initiatives. The aims of their marketplaces were much the same as the aims of the market towns of years gone by would have been—to provide well-known locations where goods and services could be traded. Figure 1-4 depicts the basic marketplace idea.

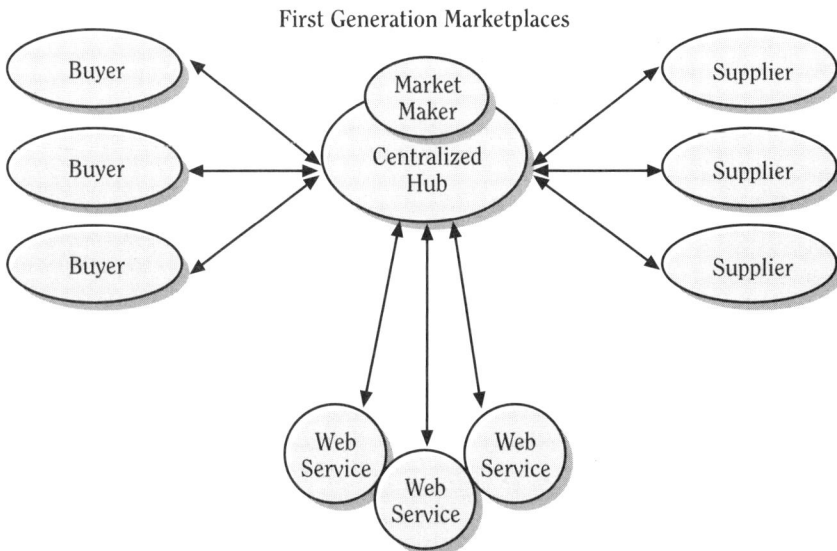

Figure 1-4. *Marketplaces emerged as a means for all suppliers and buyers to exchange goods and services for money or other value. The ability to integrate all manner of Web services with the hub allowed value to be added to the basic routing infrastructure.*

It was the turn of marketplaces, early in the year 2000, to catch the imagination of the press and the stock markets.

That Wheel Won't Spin!

Some of the marketplaces that evolved were founded on (and still operate on) truly remarkable, visionary business models. We certainly do not wish to disparage *all* marketplace initiatives, but as a whole, they were not all as successful as initially predicted. The reason for this is the same as for the automated procurement story—suppliers were not (and still are not) convinced of the value proposition that participation would bring to their companies, therefore lowering the volume of trade through the systems.

We have hinted already in this chapter that *some* marketplaces were founded on weird and wonderful business models. Such models can easily have a positive spin put on them for the purpose of press releases and other marketing campaigns. The litmus test, however, comes not in convincing the press of potential revenues, but in convincing the actual companies that need to be attracted to the marketplace that they can gain from participation.

A very simple example of the mismatch between what is generally perceived as a good proposition and what suppliers see as a poor one can be found in the levying of a transaction fee for the use of the hub. Imagine you are a marketplace operator. You prepare your business model very carefully and enter into agreements with Web service providers so that your marketplace can boast functionality for dealing with every conceivable business process that might be relevant to your buyers and suppliers. In addition to your basic message routing infrastructure, you collaborate with Web service providers to include financial services, such as consolidated payments, escrow, and credit-card authorizations. You can also boast language translations, auctioning capabilities, and calendaring, and you can even allow buyers and suppliers to implement and control shipping schedules, again by hooking up your marketplace with expert Web service providers. Your marketplace is one of the most functional available, and you have a press release detailing all of the wonderful features that you can now provide. Your public relations department states that you will make money by charging a flat fee to suppliers for all transactions that pass through your marketplace. Industry magazines need only carry out a couple of quick calculations to see two things: First, you are charging an extremely reasonable fee for the impressive range of services that you provide. Second, given the demand for such services in the B2B e-commerce arena, your company is about to make a huge amount of money. At this stage, buyer organizations are also happy because they know of the gains in efficiency that can result from streamlined procurement processes, and your solution offers that. Everyone is happy—at least while the hype is going on. Suppliers, on the other hand, analyze the proposition that your marketplace offers and decide against participation. To coin a phrase, they stay away in droves. Although this might seem strange at first, there are actually some very good reasons for this lack of participation from the suppliers' perspective.

The first question they might ask is, "Why are we being charged for a whole range of services, when we might use only a small number of them?" A good question, indeed! If a supplier simply makes use of the message routing capabilities of the hub, it is difficult to reconcile the fact that they pay the same fee as another supplier that takes advantage of consolidated payments, currency conversions, language translations, and calendaring. (In fact, even if the model is changed so that a percentage of the value of the goods being traded is used as the transaction fee, rather than a flat rate, this objection remains.)

The second question they might ask is, "How can we differentiate ourselves from our competitors in the electronic marketplace?" This is another good question. If every supplier has access to the same services and uses the same mechanisms to describe and deliver their products, one supplier can look much like another and will end up competing on price alone. Answers to this question have only evolved recently—you will read of some of the approaches that allow suppliers to differentiate their products and services later in the book. However, when the first models were being proposed, this was a major concern. Actually it is still a major concern, given that the solutions for avoiding commoditization are, as yet, by no means mature. This is one problem that you, as a supplier, must strive to understand. We will delve further into the issue of avoiding commoditization in *Chapter 2, "Business-to-Business E-Commerce Objectives for Suppliers."*

So, what seemed like a good business model had one or two fatal flaws, among others.

Note   We are not saying that all marketplaces offer poor value propositions to suppliers, but merely that, in the year 2000, there was a lot of favorable press and hype that has not been delivered on.

This sort of lesson has been, and is still being, learned by many market makers. These hard lessons have resulted in often-asked questions about whether marketplaces have any place in the future of B2B e-commerce, and if they do, what role they will play. We will attempt to answer some of these questions after our cautionary tale.

Catch 22: A Cautionary Tale

As we have emphasized before, good business strategy should always be the aim, regardless of the infrastructure that is used to undertake that business.

Business architects and decision makers should always consider the impact that their business models will have on *all* the players that they expect to participate in their initiatives. It only takes one group to refuse to participate in a market to render a business model ineffective. Hence, considering the impact on all players sounds like simple common sense. However, the failure to do this has led to the collapse of what, at first glance, seemed to be visionary ideas.

To give you a sense of the strategies behind *some* failed marketplaces, we relate the real story of a failed venture. We will withhold the names of the parties involved, but this narrative exemplifies how some seemingly good ideas can amount to nothing if the perspective of one key group is not fully accounted for. (You will not be surprised when we tell you the viewpoint of suppliers was not fully understood in this particular case.)

Our tale begins with the purchasing department of a large organization (a buyer). This company trades with more than 40,000 suppliers, so it was very interested in streamlining its procurement process. At the time, the company employed more than 1200 people in various procurement-related roles and, as such, stood to make gains that would have dwarfed the Microsoft example described earlier in this chapter.

This company was only too aware of the limitations with point-to-point procurement systems and had been following the progress of the new ideas relating to marketplaces with much interest. It seemed like a very good idea for the company to build and operate a private marketplace that would allow its suppliers to participate, using the cheap and flexible infrastructure of the Internet. Figure 1-5 shows the basis of the idea.

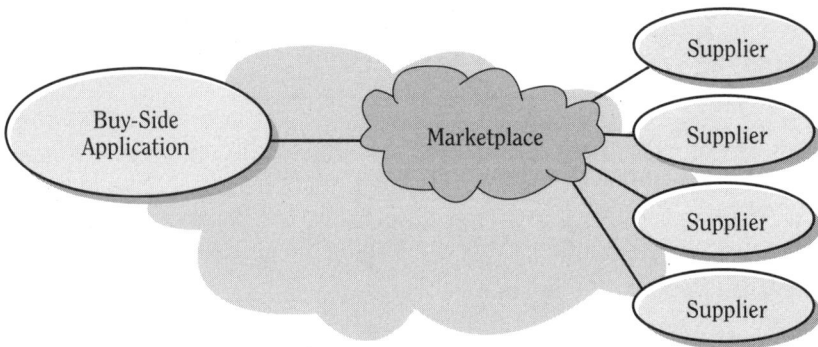

Figure 1-5.   *The starting point—a privately run marketplace. The buy-side application implemented streamlined methods for conducting procurement, but it also included other useful features for employees, such as electronic expense claim forms. The marketplace included many services that could be used in the process of B2B e-commerce.*

The company then had the idea that such a solution could be used to do more than merely streamline the procurement process for its organization. The company, along with its procurement software vendor, wanted to turn the model from just a cost-saving tool into a new source of revenue. The first idea that would help to achieve this was to resell the buy-side application to its suppliers. The aim was to have all of its suppliers using the same procurement application to achieve efficiency gains for their own procurement processes. Figure 1-6 gives you an idea of how this model was to operate.

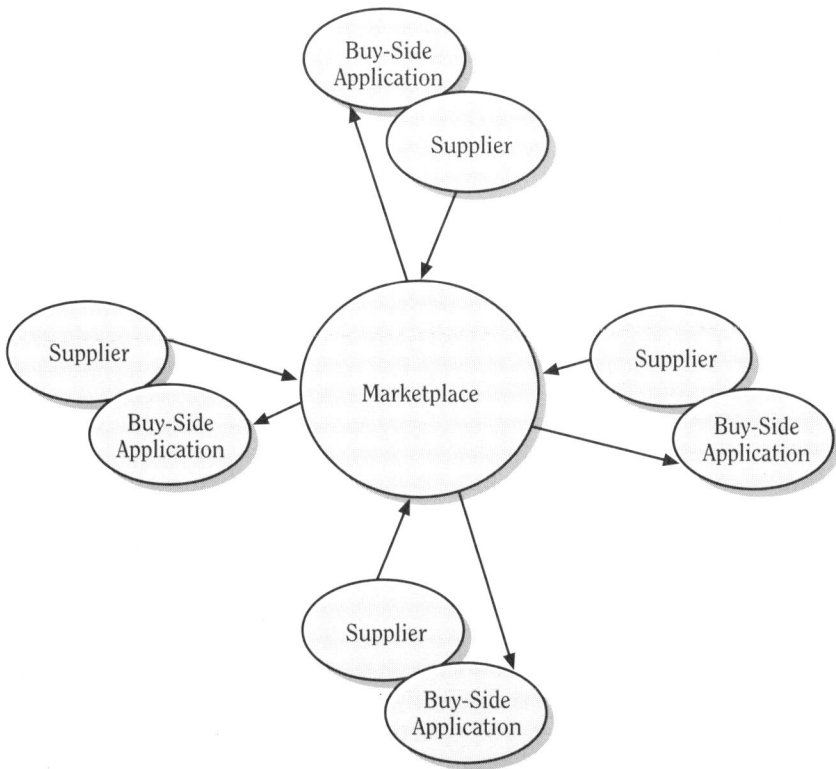

Figure 1-6.   *With every "buyer" being able to use the marketplace to sell their goods and services, and every "supplier" being able to conduct their procurement through the marketplace, a utopian model was envisaged.*

Think about all of the interactions that could have taken place through this hub. The model turned each company into a potential electronic buyer *and* supplier, so there would have been 40,000 companies trading with each other.

It was at this point that the industry press and stock markets became very excited indeed. The company proposed to charge a transaction fee of between 2 and 5 percent of the sale for all purchases made through the marketplace.

Note   We have already mentioned that charging a standard fee to suppliers for all transactions that pass through a hub, regardless of what services they used, may be viewed as inequitable. However, that perspective has only been realized in hindsight. At the time that this particular model was evolving, such issues were only just becoming apparent. We will outline other models for charging transaction fees later in this chapter.

The excitement generated was by no means unfounded. As an interesting exercise, we tried to calculate the number of transactions involved if all of the companies made one single purchase from all the other participants. That number is far too large for our spreadsheet to determine! However, that was just an interesting exercise, and of course not all companies would want (or need) to trade with all of the others. On the other hand, some companies would make thousands of purchases from some of the suppliers, so we are still talking about a number so huge as to take up far too much space in this book. Suffice to say that had this model worked, the revenue generated by the transaction fees alone would have outstripped, many times over, the income generated by the company from its traditional lines of business before this idea.

Now we need to talk about a significant flaw in this model. The initial large company enjoyed various discount deals with its suppliers. Because all other buyers would be using the same marketplace, they too would become eligible for the same discounts and benefits. Although this is a very interesting concept, consider the interaction of three companies, which we now know to be both suppliers and buyers. The first company is the initial large company. The second company is a large, global supplier of personal computers (PCs). The third company, a small organization, supplies specialty coffee blends. The initial large company purchases hundreds of PCs from our global computer supplier each year and has negotiated a good preferred discount for these purchases. Now our small coffee supplier is entitled to the same discount from the PC supplier, simply because they operate in the same marketplace. The problem is, then, that the PC supplier cannot afford to supply maybe one or two PCs per year to the coffee merchant at the same rate they offer to our large buying organization that buys thousands every year. Delivery costs, logistics, and so on, make this a bad value proposition for the PC supplier.

As a brief aside, our market maker offered consolidated payment options as one of the services provided by the hub. It reached an agreement with a financial institution that it would settle payments in a centralized manner for all transactions passing through its marketplace. In short, buyers would pay the market maker at the point of sale, and the market maker would then settle with the supplier through the arrangement with the financial institution. In reality, these payments would reside in the market maker's bank account for anything from a couple of hours to a few days. Considering that many billions of dollars could theoretically be passing through the marketplace at any one time, the interest earned by this money would amount to another large source of income. Viewed in the cold light of day, the business model proposed by our market maker really started to look like an exercise in how many different ways you can take money from suppliers. If you have read the novel *Catch-22* by Joseph Heller, you may recall that one of the characters, Milo Minderbinder, was something of an entrepreneur. His philosophy was that it is never a sin to charge as much as the market will bear. Unfortunately for *our* market maker, it attempted to take much more than suppliers would tolerate. Its marketplace barely made it past the press-release stage and was never fully implemented.

And so ends our cautionary tale. We would like to make clear that this was just one example of many different visions for how B2B e-commerce could be conducted. Some have evolved into highly successful operations, whereas others, like our example, have disappeared.

Back to Basics: Buying and Selling

You will read about many other B2B e-commerce concepts and strategies, usually from the perspective of supplier organizations, throughout the rest of this book. However, before we conclude this chapter with a discussion of the challenges your organization faces as a supplier in today's business environment, we will answer a couple of questions about marketplaces and their future roles.

Media and stock market interest in marketplaces waned over the course of 2001. Given the spectacular failures of some marketplaces, the media largely turned from a supporter of this type of initiative to a detractor. The two questions that arise from these recent events are whether marketplaces will play a role in the future of B2B e-commerce and, if so, what that role will be.

Our answer to the first question is "Yes, but…" The invention of the wheel allowed agricultural products to be moved around, and the market towns and corn exchanges provided the means of exchange that allowed the Agricultural Revolution to proceed. As for the Industrial Revolution, canals, railways, and roads provided the infrastructure that bore complex supply chains, enabling manufacturing industries to flourish. The Internet is our modern-day equivalent of the wheel or the canal. In addition to the basic infrastructure, we definitely need the means to allow businesses to trade. In effect, we need the electronic equivalent of the market town. That is the "Yes" part. We included the "but…" to qualify that marketplaces may not play such an encompassing role as was initially planned, nor should they deviate as far from the basics of good trading practices. The answer to the second question elaborates on the scope of this role.

When answering the second question, we will try to avoid too much crystal-ball gazing. Instead, we will briefly outline the current direction that market makers and previous sponsors of marketplaces are considering. The similarities between the market towns of years gone by and electronic marketplaces are beginning to emerge.

Consider a farmer bringing his livestock to market. Once in the market square, the farmer might contract the services of an auctioneer to sell the animals. He might use a lawyer in the town to produce the contracts for any exchanges. Finally, the farmer might utilize banking services to manage the payments he receives (and the payments he might make for any goods that he buys) while in town. In effect, the market town is there to enable trade. Although available in the town, the farmer has no need for the postal service or the *bureau de change*. Just because the town boasts a travel agency, that does not mean the farmer will book a vacation. In short, the farmer does not pay for all the services that the town offers—he simply pays for those amenities that he uses.

Electronic marketplaces are now starting to evolve in a similar manner to the market town. Rather than charging a flat fee to suppliers for all transactions that pass through the hub, regardless of which Web services were used, market makers are now considering simply charging for those services actually utilized in each particular instance. The marketplace will simply be the environment in which B2B e-commerce will flourish, as opposed to a specific application. Figure 1-7 compares the first generation of marketplaces with those that are beginning to emerge.

First Generation Marketplaces

Next Generation Marketplaces

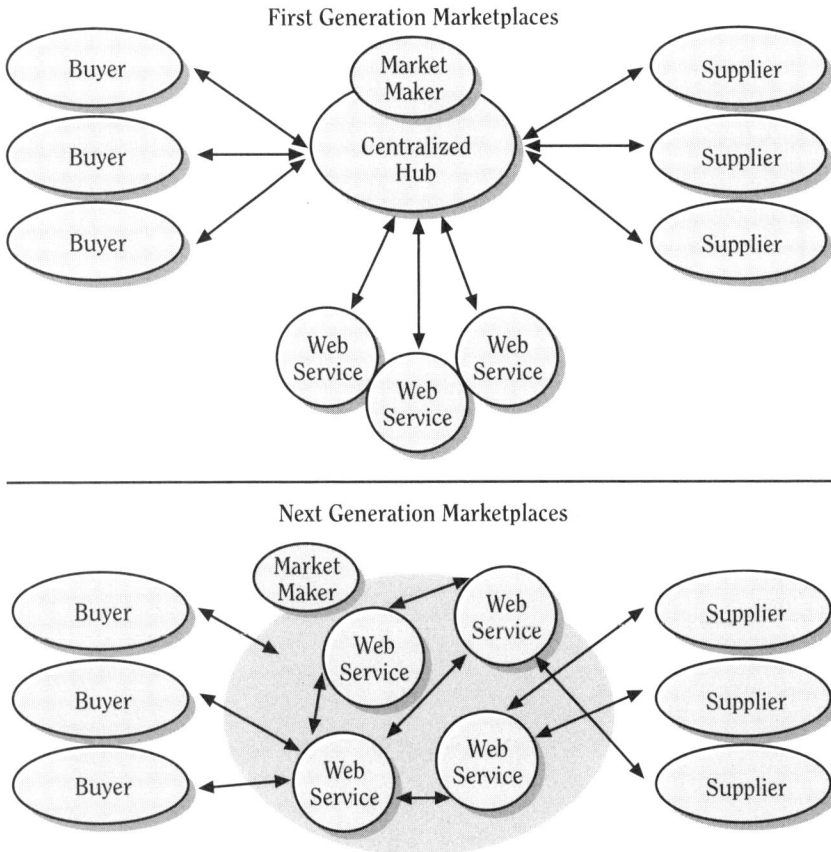

Figure 1-7.   *The first generation of marketplaces often charged suppliers a fee for transactions, regardless of which services were used, and did little to bring suppliers and buyers closer together. Suppliers saw both of these options as presenting poor value propositions. Market makers are now realizing that they should perhaps simply provide the means for efficient electronic trade between buyers and suppliers and rely on best-of-breed services to complement these relationships.*

In short, although the role that market makers will play in the future is by no means as all-encompassing as recent initiatives had planned, they nevertheless have a place in B2B e-commerce. Buyers and suppliers will have the option to use various forms of marketplaces to trade with each other as they have always done, only now in an automated manner. Both suppliers and buyers will demand the ability for suppliers to differentiate their products and services from those of competitors. The ability for both types of organizations to analyze vast amounts of business data and to base well-founded decisions on this analysis will allow them to remain empowered. In fact, they will probably be more empowered than at any time in the past—they will have the ability to react to market conditions and new opportunities much more quickly than ever before. Both buyers *and* suppliers will see the good value propositions that electronic trading can bring. Marketplaces, like other e-commerce business models, must allow for all of this if both buyers and suppliers are expected to participate in B2B e-commerce.

Challenges Facing Suppliers

Having described the various standpoints of the type of company involved in exchanging goods and services using the Internet, we will now briefly set the scene for the rest of our book.

This volume is aimed at enabling supplier organizations to sell more effectively to their business customers. Once a supplier is informed about how technology can be used to its advantage, the potential benefits far outweigh the challenges. What we will do, by way of conclusion for this chapter, is to briefly describe some of the challenges that currently face suppliers as they start interacting with their trading partners using the Internet. In *Chapter 2, "Business-to-Business E-Commerce Objectives for Suppliers,"* we will move on to discuss the objectives and benefits that suppliers can realize in this key area of their business.

Identifying Benefits to the Supplier

We have discussed the well-known benefits that buying organizations can achieve by automating their procurement processes. The overall challenge for suppliers is to identify and exploit the benefits that can be achieved by streamlining and enhancing the *selling* process. Although this pursuit is an underlying theme for this whole book, *Chapter 2, "Business-to-Business E-Commerce Objectives for Suppliers,"* describes the sort of benefits that suppliers can look to achieve by embracing B2B e-commerce, and *Chapter 3, "Technology as a Strategic Weapon for Suppliers,"* provides guidance and even a framework for evaluating the benefits that technology can bring in monetary terms.

Avoiding Poor Value Propositions

We have described some business models, largely proposed by procurement technology vendors and market makers, that provided questionable benefits for suppliers. Supplier organizations are often put under a great deal of pressure by their business customers to integrate with one system or another. As with all infrastructures, using the Internet for trading purposes will only be as successful as the business models that enable these exchanges. One key challenge for the supplier is to identify high value propositions and avoid poor ones. For example, we discuss in *Chapter 3, "Technology as a Strategic Weapon for Suppliers,"* how solutions that do not allow you to differentiate your goods and services from those of your competitors can lead to commoditization of your company and its offerings. Such solutions will undoubtedly harm your business rather than help it progress.

We are probably preaching to the converted at this point, as suppliers *have* always avoided poorly designed business models, but new models are springing up all the time. Suppliers will need to exercise their judgment carefully when choosing if and how they should participate in these new scenarios. Again, *Chapters 2* and *3* will help you separate the high-valued propositions from the poor ones.

Implementing Appropriate Solutions

Chapter 4, "Business Strategies and Solutions," and *Chapter 5, "Implementing a Solution,"* will enable you to make the transition from *assessing* the potential benefits to *choosing* your strategies and solutions for B2B e-commerce. These two chapters include case studies from several suppliers that have already implemented solutions from which they are reaping significant benefits. You will be able to learn a lot from the experiences and ideas of these real companies.

Chapter 6, "Managing the Future: Buyers, Suppliers, and B2B E-Commerce," concludes this book by providing guidance for future-proofing your strategies in what is an inherently unpredictable area. Although we are no better at looking into the future than you are, we do provide some advice for safeguarding your investment in B2B e-commerce.

In short, the rest of this book will help you to overcome the challenges that you face as a supplier participating in B2B e-commerce.

Summary: Supplier Participation in B2B E-Commerce

As we discussed earlier, the complexities of B2B e-commerce can sometimes seem bewildering. Hopefully, you now have a good feel for the nature of modern B2B e-commerce. You should now understand those issues that we feel are particularly important for suppliers as you read the rest of this book.

Because we are effectively in the middle of the Information Revolution, things will undoubtedly change. However, this is no reason to avoid making the most of the Internet for trading purposes as soon as a good value proposition appears. In fact, if you do not take advantage of such opportunities to streamline and improve your selling processes, your company may not be well positioned to adapt to the changes that are certain to come.

Perhaps the one key idea that you should take with you as you delve into the chapters that follow is that trading electronically is all about communication. Being able to exchange the vast amounts of information that underpin all modern trading practices is the way in which your business will thrive. The Internet allows that exchange in an efficient, relatively inexpensive, and flexible manner.

Given that B2B e-commerce is a relatively new idea, the process of the shift in trading practices has seen both successes and failures. The cause of the failures is rooted largely in questionable business models. Successful ventures, on the other hand, have been able to combine technology with sound business practices. Your goal, as a supplier wishing to move your trading practices into the Information Age, must be to identify successful models and utilize those for the benefit of your company.

Trading has been essential to the survival of our species and will obviously continue to be so. Using the Internet to conduct trade in an efficient manner is essential to the survival of your business.

Business-to-Business E-Commerce Objectives for Suppliers

We might do well to inquire about the nature of a supplier's business. What is it, in itself? What are the first principles of the selling process? What specific need do we serve by selling? At this level, suppliers are in business to trade goods and services for money. All else is incidental.

As a supplier of goods or services to other businesses, your company operates within a certain framework. It probably participates in a supply chain of one type or another. That framework is underpinned by communication between your organization and your trading partners. Communication between businesses has traditionally been achieved using a number of different mechanisms, such as postal services, couriers, telephone networks, in-person interaction, fax machines, and, more recently, e-mail systems. Today, businesses are looking to extend their use of the Internet to create a more powerful way of communicating with other companies. However, the sole reason for doing this is to support the trade of goods and services for money.

Many business decision makers do not feel constrained by the communication mechanisms their company uses—they develop strategies for building business relationships, selling more of their goods and services, and moving their company forward. The mechanisms used for communication while building and evolving these relationships are not usually a major concern. If you stand back and analyze what is really happening, however, the business decision makers *are* actually constrained by how communication between organizations really takes place. For example, decision makers might decide that their company needs to provide postsales support for a certain product. They might compare costs associated with employee time spent in dealing with customers against the benefits derived from this additional support, such as increased sales, better customer relationships, and repeat orders from satisfied customers. They are unlikely, however, to consider factors such as employees being away from their telephones for one reason or another, industrial action by postal services, or delays in courier services. However, these factors *do* affect businesses on a daily basis.

We are not saying that companies are ignorant of these factors, but rather that these issues are so deeply ingrained in the way that companies communicate with each other that they are simply accepted. The reality is that companies have become so used to operating within the constraints imposed by the traditional ways of doing business that those constraints have become a given. People accept the limitations of traditional communication mechanisms and then implement strategies within that framework. Decision makers have become conditioned to working within the environment that has characterized business-to-business (B2B) trading for many decades.

You will have gathered by now that we are specifically interested in how you can use the infrastructure of the Internet to exchange the data required to do business with your trading partners. Further, we consider that the Internet offers fantastic opportunities for improving your business and its processes. Buyers will be able to make more dynamic choices about which suppliers they use, regardless of where those suppliers are located, and suppliers will be able to expose the full value proposition that they offer, including rich product information, pre- and postsales support, advice on how best to use their offerings, and so on. Strategic relationships can be built between buyers and suppliers, and both types of organizations will be able to analyze their business data in a useful and timely manner, allowing them to react quickly and decisively to changes in market conditions.

Note   The Internet is sometimes described as providing the basis for what economists term the *perfect market*. However, this is inaccurate because the perfect market concept is founded on many principles that do not apply to our business environment, Internet-based or otherwise. For example, the perfect market operates in conditions where no trade barriers exist, the buying and selling of any goods or services are deemed to be legal, and all resources are privately owned. There are many additional conditions that need to be met before a market is considered perfect in terms of economic theory. We prefer to think of the Internet as offering opportunities for a *better* market than before, where businesses are more agile, communication is more effective, processes are less error-prone, and inefficiencies are reduced.

If you are serious about improving the sell-side of your business by using the Internet to communicate with your trading partners, you can no longer ignore the communication mechanism itself when you are developing your business strategies. The whole point of using the Internet for B2B trading purposes is that you can now implement strategies that were not possible a few years ago. Rather than simply accepting the effects that communication mechanisms have on the way your company operates, you must now actively consider how these mechanisms influence your business plans. A positive way to look at this is that you can now gain advantages from the new ways of communicating and collaborating with your trading partners. At the very least, you can remove many inefficiencies in your business processes. At the other end of the scale, you can revolutionize the way in which you conduct business by developing new strategies that work specifically over the Internet.

It is probably the very newness of the infrastructure that demands that you look carefully at all issues surrounding communication with other organizations over the Internet. Although we prefer not to predict the future, we can easily envision a situation, in a few years, when once again business decision makers can develop business strategies without too much thought about the communication processes involved. Using the Internet as the means of communication will be the norm, and you will simply make decisions in that particular framework, much as you have done in recent years. However, the use of the Internet is in a transitional period as we write this book, and not all the issues surrounding this communication mechanism have yet been ironed out. Our aim in this book is to help you make a transition of your own—moving your company into the Information Age and allowing you to use the Internet for selling your goods and services more effectively.

As we already discussed in *Chapter 1, "The Role of Suppliers in Business-to-Business E-Commerce,"* using the Internet to exchange business data, such as purchase orders, invoices, and so on, is still a relatively new idea. The infrastructure and ideas about how to conduct business using that communication mechanism are still evolving. Some of the first ideas proved to be poor value propositions for supplier organizations. In fact, the basic flaw in most of those models was that suppliers would no longer be able to exercise the freedom they have traditionally enjoyed when making decisions about how they conduct their business. Their control over how they would make money could have been diminished had they participated in some of the initiatives that recently characterized B2B e-commerce.

In this chapter, we discuss the concept of supplier empowerment as it relates to trading with other businesses over the Internet. Remaining within this context, we will outline the objectives that all suppliers look to achieve as they participate in B2B e-commerce. We conclude this chapter with a brief discussion of realizing those business objectives in today's B2B e-commerce environment. Subsequent chapters will delve deeper into using technology solutions to achieve those objectives.

What Is Supplier Empowerment?

We use the term *supplier empowerment* to represent the idea that your company can utilize the infrastructure of the Internet to sell your goods and services more effectively and provide a better experience for your business customers, while using your internal strengths to retain control over the core information and processes of your business. To remain empowered, you must be able to make decisions about the directions your company should take, and you must be able to steer your business in those directions. You must not be restricted in the control you exercise over your company's strategies by the infrastructure that you use to communicate with your trading partners. Instead, you should look to use the Internet to your advantage by exercising your core strengths in the best ways for your customers. Now, more than at any time in the past, these opportunities are available.

To remain empowered, you must be able to use technology in ways that improve your overall business (benefiting both you and your customers), rather than as a way to simply comply with customer needs in a tactical way. As we have recounted already, suppliers have been avoiding poor value propositions from buyers and market makers, and rightly so. The challenge is to be able to identify and participate in *high* value propositions. For example, you might identify a number of customers that are important enough to your business that you want to integrate directly with their automated procurement systems or marketplaces. You might then conclude that the manner in which you present your goods and services needs to be tailored for each of these channels. When selling through electronic marketplaces, you might want to offer discounts to those companies with whom you trade directly, whereas you might want to more heavily advertise related goods and services with every sale you make in a public marketplace. Of course, these are just some examples of what a supplier might want—the exact strategies that you build are up to you. The key point is that you retain control, sell more effectively, and differentiate your goods and services for competitive advantage.

The good news is that the technology for achieving such goals is now available and solutions based on this technology are rapidly maturing. The direction in which these solutions are evolving has been influenced by the lack of supplier participation in B2B e-commerce to date—vendors of these solutions are now addressing the issues that face suppliers out of necessity. As we know, without active supplier participation, B2B e-commerce would amount to very little.

From a supplier's perspective, there has never been a better time to start embracing the Internet and technology solutions as a serious approach to how you interact with your customers. Business models are now emerging that allow you to differentiate your goods and services from those of your competitors and, additionally, sell effectively to many business customers through numerous electronic selling channels, thereby allowing you to maintain and improve your market agility. Compare this to some of the earlier models that we outlined in *Chapter 1, "The Role of Suppliers in Business-to-Business E-Commerce,"* and you will no doubt understand that this is a far more attractive approach for online traders. Along with these business models, sell-side e-commerce technology has also been evolving. Solutions now exist that really *will* allow you to accomplish these objectives with very little effort or extra investment.

Supplier Business Objectives

Chapter 4, "Business Strategies and Solutions," and *Chapter 5, "Implementing a Solution,"* will guide you through the process of matching strategies and solutions to your business needs. For now, we discuss the business objectives that can be achieved by embracing B2B e-commerce from the perspective of supplier organizations.

Improving Your Bottom Line

At the beginning of this chapter, we stated that making money is a key aspect of being in business as a supplier. What we are ultimately talking about is making monetary profit from selling goods and services. Although many different key stakeholders in your company may have intermediate goals other than achieving the desired level of profit, this is what it all comes down to. Even though the chief operating officer (COO) may be interested specifically in reducing operational costs, and the chief executive officer (CEO) may continuously strive to increase shareholder dividends, the overall goal of making a profit remains. If the chief financial officer (CFO) seems preoccupied with return on investment (ROI) predictions, that is understandable. The reason, however, that all of these stakeholders take interest in such things is they all ultimately tie in with the bottom line on the balance sheet: profit.

Many factors affect the generation of profit. Some of these factors, such as revenue and costs, directly affect the balance sheet. Other factors, many of which are unique to your company, indirectly affect profits by influencing the amount of revenue or the level of cost. Typical examples of such influences include operational efficiency, sales and marketing agility, cost of sales, and the strength of your customer relationships. We discuss these factors in the context of supplier empowerment in B2B e-commerce.

Increasing Revenue

One of the most obvious ways to positively affect your company's balance sheet is to strive for increased revenue. Of course, increased revenues can often be achieved with no net gain to the company. If increases were only achievable by incurring costs that could never be matched by the revenue gained, only an unwise business decision maker would advocate that approach. We will discuss costs next, but for the moment we focus on the fact that most companies continually strive to increase their sales revenue. The issue is how this can be achieved and maximized in the B2B e-commerce world.

Increased revenues can be achieved in a number of ways. One is to simply make more sales. To achieve this, you could persuade your existing customers to buy more of your products at the current price, perhaps with a marketing campaign or a concerted sales effort. Alternatively, you could try to attract new customers while retaining your existing ones, again keeping prices constant. On the other hand, you could decrease prices to aid in your attempts to both sell more to existing customers *and* attract new business. You would, of course, have to be careful that the increase in units sold would be more than enough to offset the decreased unit price if you adopted such a strategy. Additionally, you might add extra value of one kind or another to what you offer so that buyers can differentiate between your goods and services and those supplied by your competitors, thereby helping your sales effort.

On the other hand, you might calculate that *increasing* prices, in certain circumstances, can result in higher profits. You may well lose some customers with this approach, but the increased revenue from those customers who continue to buy from you, along with reduced customer service costs, may be more than enough to offset the lost sales volume.

All of these approaches are traditional business strategies. You will undoubtedly use the ones most appropriate for your business—we are not attempting to influence your sales strategy here. There are many variations on these techniques for increasing sales, but discussing them here is not our goal. What we *do* wish to convey to you now is that you can maximize the return on your existing sales strategies, whatever they might be, by taking advantage of the Internet and B2B e-commerce technologies.

Another example of how technology can aid your sales effort is that your customers will find purchasing from you a much more attractive proposition if they can do so efficiently and in collaborative ways. We have already discussed the vast savings that can be achieved by buyers using automated procurement systems. Sometimes the idea of suppliers integrating with these systems is so important to buyers that they limit or even refuse to do business with suppliers that will not trade electronically. We do not necessarily advise buyers to take this stance, but such sentiments *are* being conveyed to many suppliers, even as we write this book. Making the process of buying from your company easy and efficient will only reinforce your efforts to keep existing customers. Moreover, it will be a definite aid in your pursuit of new customers and new revenue from existing customers.

Gaining new customers is often constrained by how many you can feasibly reach and communicate with effectively. The ability to interact with electronic procurement systems is an excellent way to accelerate those new relationships. Registering with new online registry services such as Universal Description, Discovery, and Integration (UDDI; see sidebar) and selling via electronic marketplaces can be additional ways to showcase your goods and services to an even wider audience of buyers. If you can compete and operate effectively in these arenas, you will find that customers you may have never heard of, let alone attempted to sell to, will be more attracted to your business. Supplier-centric solutions that allow integration with a wide variety of procurement systems, as well as marketplaces and other selling channels, now exist.

Universal Description, Discovery, and Integration (UDDI)

UDDI (*www.uddi.org*) is a set of standards that defines how companies can expose the functionality of their business applications as Web services. As such, UDDI makes it easier for businesses to participate in B2B e-commerce. It specifies how an organization can expose applications (such as order management, procurement, marketing, inventory, and billing systems) so that other companies can integrate with them over the Internet. Because UDDI involves a standardized way for describing how other businesses can integrate with your systems, it allows your business customers, suppliers, and other trading partners to interact more easily with your company.

(continued)

> **Universal Description, Discovery, and Integration (UDDI)** *(continued)*
>
> In addition, UDDI defines and maintains registries, such as *www.uddi.microsoft.com,* that contain the profiles of many businesses and Web services. You can think of these UDDI registries as a type of automated, electronic business white pages. These registries are Internet directories of businesses and the applications that they have exposed for use in B2B e-commerce and other scenarios. Applications can use a UDDI registry to find companies and their applications, much as a person might use a Web search engine to find Web sites, but in an automated manner. This automated application-to-application discovery eliminates many of the compatibility and configuration problems that are commonly encountered in the B2B arena, and it also becomes a means of selling to customers who have obtained your details from these registries.

In short, increasing revenues through increased sales is one of the primary motives for suppliers to start trading in the online world. Although we have painted a rather rosy picture at this point, be aware that the very process of selling online raises its own issues, such as how to differentiate your company from competitors in your market, and how to expose the true value of your goods and services, rather than just displaying basic information and prices. We will address these, and other issues, later.

Decreasing Costs

As already mentioned, revenue is not the only component that affects the bottom line of the balance sheet. Because of its effect on profit, decreasing costs is also a widely sought-after goal.

In *Chapter 1, "The Role of Suppliers in Business-to-Business E-Commerce,"* we discussed how Microsoft effected a reduction in the average transaction cost of making a purchase from around $65 to somewhere between $5 and $10. Over the course of a year, this amounted to cost savings of approximately $30 million. This reduction in transaction costs was largely achieved using its automated procurement system, MS Market, to eliminate the time-consuming processes of manual, paper-based purchasing. This paperwork, before MS Market, included purchase orders, invoices, delivery slips, payments, receipts, and so on. MS Market, and other procurement systems, deal with this data electronically. The data is exchanged quickly and efficiently between Microsoft and its trading partners.

Given that dealing with data of this nature is not restricted to the buying organization but must also be dealt with by suppliers, there is a strong argument that supplier organizations can achieve reductions in transaction costs that are comparable in magnitude to those of their customers. The only difference is one of perspective: buyers look to achieve reductions in the transaction cost of making purchases, whereas suppliers look for similar reductions in making sales. Buyers aim to automate the creation and transmission of purchase orders, the receipt and processing of invoices, the sending of payments, and the management of receipts. Suppliers, on the other hand, look to receive and process purchase orders, create and send invoices, receive payment notifications, and generate and send receipts. In short, if buyers can achieve massive reductions in transaction costs by dealing with this data in an automated manner, then so can suppliers.

A reduction in transaction costs is not the only saving suppliers can realize by embracing B2B e-commerce. Costs not directly associated with processing sales can also be reduced. For example, providing comprehensive presales information in an easy-to-access, online format can reduce the cost of dealing with customer inquiries, even before you start exchanging the business documents that underpin the selling process. Similarly, making postsales support available online can reduce the costs associated with providing valuable assistance to your customers after a sale has ended.

Another example of reducing costs, other than those directly associated with sales transactions, can be found in marketing campaigns. An online campaign can be less expensive and more effective than traditional approaches to marketing. You will be able to use data collected from previous sales (and other interactions with your customers) to construct the foundations of your campaigns. This makes the process of delivering highly targeted advertisements and other information much more soundly based than it often appears in the traditional business environment. On a related topic, the very fact that you, as a business decision maker, can analyze vast amounts of information effectively (if it is collected and stored in an appropriate format), means that the processes involved in developing your business strategies can be more efficient, and therefore less costly.

These examples of cost savings that can be achieved by automating your selling process are just a few among many. Your company might realize any number of cost-saving practices that will be particular to your business. Suffice it to say, savings that can be made by suppliers automating the sell-side of their businesses should at least be comparable to those made by buyers that automate the buy-side of this equation. There is even an argument that suppliers will be able to reduce costs in many more areas of their business than buyers. Sell-side solutions already exist that allow you to reduce all of the costs that we have mentioned. Such costs include those associated directly with order processing and indirect costs such as advertising and marketing, as well as many others.

Improving Efficiency

We have already discussed, in the previous section, how increasing efficiency in the selling process can directly reduce the transaction costs of making those sales. Rather than going over the same ground here, we discuss another, perhaps more important effect that improving efficiency can have on your business.

You may recall, again from our procurement example in *Chapter 1, "The Role of Suppliers in Business-to-Business E-Commerce,"* that Microsoft, as a buyer, considered the reduction in transaction costs for purchasing goods to be a secondary benefit of their automated procurement system. They viewed the *time* saved by *all* employees as the most important effect. This determination was made on the basis that the company is a knowledge-based organization, and employees are paid to use their knowledge and time constructively in moving the business forward. Your company, as a supplier, can realize similar benefits. Rather than being bogged down in the paperwork that underpins your selling process, your employees can use their time more constructively. Your sales team can concentrate on what they are good at, namely communicating with and selling to your customers. However, it is not only sales staff that have had to manage too much paperwork in recent years. Almost all parts of a modern company come into contact, at one point or another, with paperwork or manual processes that are directly or indirectly involved in the sales process. For example, managers might need to authorize concessionary deals for a certain customer, or approve a given sales and marketing initiative, and your warehouse workers might need to deal with paper-based purchase orders if you are a supplier of physical goods. Removing inefficiencies in the selling process by automating those tasks that have traditionally been paper-based means that your managers can spend more time managing and your warehouse workers can spend more time working with your inventory.

In short, most employees will be able to carry out their primary roles much more efficiently if your selling process is automated. The effect on the bottom line might well be greater from this single concept than from all the other factors combined!

Reducing Errors

Most supply-oriented companies experience errors from time to time when their staff manually processes orders. These errors may occur for a number of reasons, but typographical errors as employees enter details into order-entry systems are common to many businesses. Entering details of orders received by fax, e-mail, or regular mail is an inherently error-prone process. Many suppliers even have their staff print out order information received via electronic data interchange (EDI) systems and then rekey that data into their order-entry systems. This process is particularly prone to errors because EDI data is not often easily interpreted by people.

Other occurrences that can be counted as errors include paper-based orders being discarded accidentally, misunderstanding as to which particular staff member would process a certain order, and so on.

Regardless of the causes of error in the manual order-processing procedures at your company, you can be sure of one thing: these errors result in lost sales. A substantial risk is that not only the order that was mislaid or entered incorrectly will be lost, but that buyers will become disenchanted with your company if such errors occur repeatedly. If that happens, as it unfortunately does from time to time, you will risk losing the many repeat orders that buyer could have placed in the future. We are sure you know how difficult it is to gain new customers, so the last thing that any supplier wants is to damage existing customer relationships.

On top of losing specific orders, and even customers, errors in order processing represent a significant amount of wasted effort. It is a complete waste of time (and money) for your employees to process an order, only for an error to render that time worthless in terms of generating revenue for your company.

With the best efforts in the world, and even the most conscientious order-entry staff, errors will always occur in the process of manual data entry. Such errors can be all but eliminated by automating the order capture and processing area of your business with intelligent software. *Buyers* can still make errors, such as ordering an inappropriate quantity of a given product, but at least your company will not have caused the error. You are unlikely to risk losing business from such a company if the error originated with them.

In summary, the bottom line on your company's balance sheet is affected by many different factors, both direct and indirect. Increasing revenue and reducing costs are obvious objectives that you will want to achieve as you enter the world of B2B e-commerce. Remember, however, that automating your business processes can have many other positive, but indirect, effects on the well-being of your company: you can achieve a reduction in errors, better relationships with your customers, and a more efficient and useful workforce, along with a streamlined, automated business.

Remaining Empowered

It is time to think strategically. Although you can migrate your traditional business strategies to the B2B e-commerce arena, this change can resurrect issues that you might once have solved, in the context of traditional business, years earlier. You will need to devise business plans that tackle these issues, this time in the context of B2B e-commerce.

This change also provides new opportunities for how you can strategically place your company within the B2B e-commerce framework. We will delve further into this concept in *Chapter 3, "Technology as a Strategic Weapon for Suppliers."*

Next, we discuss the objectives that will enable your company to remain empowered as you start to sell your products and services to your business customers over the Internet.

Avoiding Commoditization

Very few suppliers want to compete on price alone. Where companies *are* forced to do so, we often see slim profit margins and a struggle to maintain market share. In fact, profit may even drop into negative figures as companies adopt loss-leader strategies. That may sound like good news for customers, but it is certainly not a lasting strategy for most suppliers. Remember our first principle from the beginning of this chapter: suppliers must make a profit to stay in business. In fact, such conditions do not actually benefit even the buyers. Suppliers that could have offered excellent service, and even become important strategic business partners for the buyer organization, will have ceased trading long before such benefits can be reaped.

We briefly examine the world of retailing to the general public so that we can discuss the simplest type of sale, in this case an individual buying a can of baked beans from a supermarket. Many brands of beans are available at the supermarket. The product really *is* a commodity, because similar cans of beans exist. Supermarkets and suppliers, however, try to avoid presenting even baked beans as such; instead, they become particularly inventive in building relationships with their customers and showing added value. They aim to communicate with their customers so that those individuals see extra value, such as quality and customer service, in buying a particular brand. All in all, the supplier's objective is to *avoid* the situation in which their customers see their can of baked beans as just a commodity.

Considering that even the simplest sale of a real commodity is rarely presented as such, you will see how much more important it is to emphasize the true value of your own goods and services to your customers. Whatever your line of business, there are undoubtedly many factors that you believe make your company a more attractive supplier than your competitors. Even if you are still working on improving this aspect of your business, you will want to be able to communicate these advantages to your buyers. (If you think that your company doesn't offer good value at present, and won't in the future, it might be time to consider changing jobs!)

Although the discussion about avoiding commoditization is not a new one, it is an issue that you will need to revisit as you enter the world of B2B e-commerce. You will often find that you are competing in an environment where you cannot rely on a good pitch from your sales executives, pointing out the benefits of buying from your company, on a one-to-one basis in person or over the telephone. In fact, you can lose potential buyers long before you were aware that they existed. Your objectives, therefore, should include ensuring that buyers can differentiate between your product offerings and those of your competitors as they make electronic purchases. You can achieve this by ensuring that rich product (or service) information is available to customers at the point of sale.

Along with providing rich information that ensures your customers can differentiate your products and services from those of your competitors, you can aim to avoid commoditization in a number of other ways:

- **Strengthening your brand.** Rather than losing your corporate identity as you participate in B2B e-commerce, your objectives should be to use the Internet to *strengthen* your brand, thereby allowing your customers to more readily associate high value with your company.

- **Allowing configuration and customization.** You should also consider allowing your customers to configure (where appropriate) what they are purchasing. The ability to customize your products and services so that they meet the exact needs of the buyer will help build customer loyalty.

- **Providing personalization.** Another way to build customer loyalty is to present buyers with a personalized experience when they purchase from you. Not only can you allow the buyers themselves to configure the purchasing process so that it best suits them, you can also use the data generated by their previous actions to automatically present them with tailored information in the future. The more they interact with you, the better the information and options will be suited to their needs.

We will talk about the basic functionality that your company will require to avoid commoditization when we guide you through matching solutions to your strategies in *Chapter 4, "Business Strategies and Solutions,"* and *Chapter 5, "Implementing a Solution."*

Improving Market Agility

Another slant on remaining empowered is being able to adapt your business strategies as and when *you* see fit, rather than being constrained by technological or communication barriers. You will want to adapt your strategies both to react to market conditions and to implement more proactive plans, as you guide your company forward. You should be able to implement any new or modified business strategies quickly and effectively for your existing customers and use this ability to attract and sell effectively to new ones.

A common goal of most suppliers as they participate in B2B e-commerce is to sell through multiple channels. This, like reducing costs, increasing revenues, and avoiding commoditization, is not a new business idea. Rather, it is an objective that you will need to address in the new context of B2B e-commerce. As with all those other issues, your challenge is to transform your traditional strategies for controlling how, when, and where you sell your goods and services so that they are effective in the Internet environment.

Another way to remain agile, in the context of sell-side B2B e-commerce, centers on your ability to take advantage of the many new electronic sales channels (such as automated procurement systems and marketplaces) without having to restructure the automated sell-side of your business. If new customers emerge with electronic trading capabilities, you should be able to add them to your existing environment with minimal effort or cost. If a new business informs you that it would like to use you as a preferred supplier as long as you can integrate with its procurement system, you should not have to lose sleep worrying about how you will integrate with this company. On the other hand, if a certain marketplace is offering what turns out to be a poor value proposition to your company, you may want the ability to disengage quickly and easily. Having one system that can manage these changes is critical. Figure 2-1 shows how a customer can deal with multiple customers through multiple sales channels.

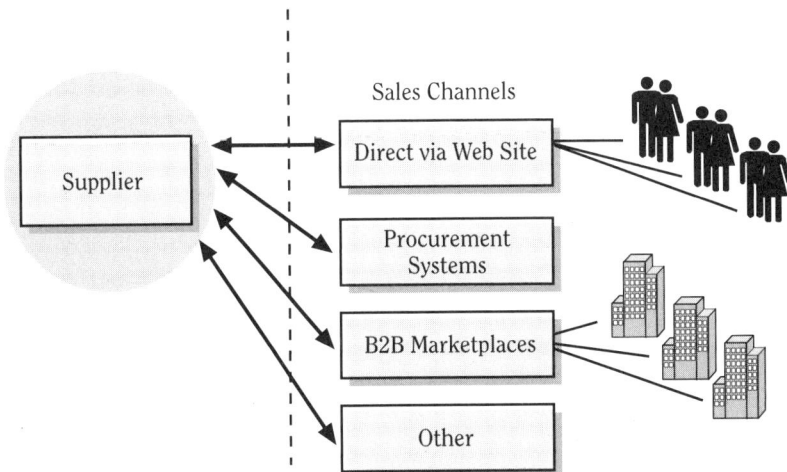

Figure 2-1.   *To maximize your agility as a supplier, it is important that you understand the various ways in which your customers can buy from you. In additon, you need to ensure that your e-commerce strategy and solutions are able to adapt to new customer requirements and new channels rapidly.*

Of course, you should ensure that your business strategies for how, when, and where you sell your goods and services are all based on the firmest possible ground. Business intelligence and decision-support systems can help you achieve this—not only will you be more agile in the electronic world, but any moves you make will be more sound than ever before.

Making Good Business Decisions

Data analysis systems exist to answer business questions. Now, there are many questions you might ask of your business. Some of these are operational questions such as, "Has customer *xxx* settled invoice number *yyy* yet?" or "Have we received that shipment from supplier *zzz*?" Other questions certainly have more of a strategic basis that needs to be addressed to move your business forward. Examples of this type of question would be, "What is the relationship between sales of product A and those of product B?" and "What characteristics distinguish customers that typically buy our top-of-the-line products from those that traditionally buy our midpriced goods?" A simpler question (at least from the perspective of the IT staff who will have to extract the answer from a database) might be, "What was the total value of our sales in the Northeast region last year, and how does that compare to our performance in the Northwest?" So, we will rephrase our initial statement: data analysis systems exist to answer *strategic* business questions.

Operational questions are best answered by operational systems. Whether a certain customer has settled a particular invoice is easily answered by your accounting system. Whether a given shipment has been received from a certain supplier is best answered by your inventory system. Operational systems, however, cannot usually answer the more complex strategic questions—they are not designed to expose relationships between the sales of certain products, and they will not provide answers about the characteristics of certain customer behaviors. In some cases, they *can* answer the simpler type of strategic questions, such as providing basic aggregates of sales figures. However, the response time for presenting this type of answer is often not acceptable—because, for example, IT staff may have to construct specific database queries, and computers often take a long time to resolve this type of query. Overall, however, strategic questions are best answered by analytical systems.

The basic reason for needing specific analysis systems is twofold. First, they can provide the complex insight into your business that your operational systems cannot. Second, they can answer certain questions quickly and easily, questions that would otherwise involve a lot of effort (both by IT staff and computers) for your operational systems to resolve.

You might well have been benefiting from sophisticated decision-support systems for many years now in areas other than B2B e-commerce. However, analyzing data generated from your business interactions on the Internet raises a few new issues, and more opportunities as well.

Bringing the Internet to the Warehouse

As you begin to sell to your trading partners over the Internet, you will find that an unprecedented amount of information is generated, and can be captured, from your business interactions. You will have access to *clickstream* data that represents the behavior of your customers as they browse your catalogs and place orders. This data goes a lot further than simply describing completed orders. It can show you which other goods or services customers looked at (but did not buy) in conjunction with those that they actually bought. It can detail the actions taken by a customer backing out of a purchase partially through the procurement process. It can trace the trajectory of customer actions as they search for more details about your value as a supplier. In short, you can access information that will allow you to not only analyze your sales figures, but also completely analyze the behavior of customers as they interact in your sales process.

In addition to analyzing data by customer, you will also be able to gain insight into the characteristics of your different sales *channels*. For example, you can compare how customers make purchases through procurement systems with how they buy from marketplaces or place orders directly on your Web site. All of this, of course, is invaluable information that you can use in your short-term tactics and long-term strategies.

If you sell your goods and services through a sophisticated sell-side application, this, too, can provide similar details. Further, it can include information from the buy-side applications used by your customers. Examination of the buy-side information can help to improve the processes that *your customers'* employees undertake as they buy from you. What more evidence do buyers need that they can usefully work with your company?

In short, the Internet offers a much larger, richer source of information about the behaviors of your business customers than has ever been available before. You should take full advantage of this unprecedented opportunity for analyzing and improving your business.

Leveraging Your Existing IT Investments

Compared to the exciting concepts of using data analysis systems to make faster and more intelligent decisions, a discussion of integrating with your existing IT investments may seem mundane. Nevertheless, this is also a critical objective that you should consider carefully as you prepare your strategies for selling online.

Integrating with Internal Systems

As you build your strategy for embracing B2B e-commerce, one important objective is that any new system must integrate within your existing IT environment. For example, you may have one or more existing enterprise resource planning (ERP) systems that allow the different parts of your business to function coherently, smoothly, and effectively. Such systems may tie together departments such as accounting, purchasing, manufacturing, product development, customer service, and sales by allowing them to cooperate. You will certainly not want to disrupt the smooth operation of your company by introducing a new system that does not integrate with and—more important—leverage such an important cornerstone of your business.

Integrating with Your Suppliers

Just as you will want to ensure that your B2B strategy integrates with your internal IT solutions, such as ERP systems, you will also want to be certain that your initiative will not negatively affect, or even destroy, your relationships with *your* suppliers. For example, you may currently use some type of supply-chain management (SCM) system to optimize the flow of products or information so that one step in your business process flows seamlessly into the next. Your suppliers will probably make a significant contribution to this flow, and you will not want to interrupt that. Alternatively, your suppliers may be implementing their own sell-side solutions for the same reasons that you are. You should ensure that the critical link between your suppliers and your company is intact as *you* start selling online. Remember that suppliers have been avoiding poor value propositions (hence the need for this book)—you should not forget that the success of your suppliers is directly tied to your success, specifically when trading online.

Managing the Impact on Your Staff

Your staff may have become comfortable using your existing IT infrastructure for various tasks. They will be familiar with your order-entry systems, your reporting systems, your ERP solutions, and so on. The introduction of a new system, no matter how easy it is to use, is often met with some resistance.

One of the key aspects to a successful project is to involve as many of the people who will use the new systems as possible in the design process. One of the positive aspects of this approach is that resistance can be minimized with broader involvement. Also, soliciting the input of these people will often result in a solution that does exactly what is required. In fact, one or more specific representatives of the business should be involved all the way through the development process to ensure that it meets the users' needs at every stage. Finally, comprehensive training programs should be provided for the staff that will directly interact with any new system, including those responsible for maintaining it.

Realizing Your Business Objectives

As you devise your strategy for selling online, you will need to know how to realize your business objectives. In *Chapter 4, "Business Strategies and Solutions," and Chapter 5, "Implementing a Solution,"* we will delve into details about the different types of solutions available to you and how to ensure that you can achieve exactly what you need from these systems. For now, we provide a brief outline of what you will be looking for as you attempt to achieve the business objectives we have outlined so far.

Making Products and Services Available

Starting with the very basics, you will need to make the information that describes your products and services available online, so good catalog design and easy management of the information in that catalog are absolute necessities. Your catalog is your showcase for presenting the types of goods and services you provide. Being able to present this information as you see fit is essential. Depending on how you wish to participate in B2B e-commerce models, you may need to deliver custom catalogs for use by specific customers or through specific channels, such as your Web site, marketplaces, and so on.

Quite simply, the ability to present well-designed, manageable catalogs can make a significant contribution to your objective of increasing revenue. You will find that you have a much larger base of potential customers than ever before, and you will also be seen as an attractive proposition from the perspective of buyer organizations that want to conduct their procurement process in an automated manner.

Additionally, being able to showcase your products and services in an automated manner can significantly decrease costs involved in the selling process. If your product information is well organized, easily searchable, and sufficiently detailed, costs associated with customer service can be reduced and customer satisfaction will increase.

Receiving Business Orders

Publishing catalog information and receiving orders usually go hand in hand, as you might expect. You can match the automation of this side of your business against some of your most important business objectives. You will realize a reduction in costs associated with order processing, and the efficiency gains from reductions in the amount of paperwork that your employees have traditionally undertaken will be substantial. Remember, not only will the staff directly involved with order processing become more efficient, but everyone from your business managers to your warehouse staff will be able to concentrate on what they do best, rather than being bogged down with the paperwork involved in the sales process.

Another business objective that can be achieved by an automated order-receipt process is that errors associated with the manual input of order details can be reduced, if not eradicated.

Beyond Catalog Publishing

It is tempting to think that all your objectives have been addressed by publishing catalogs and receiving orders—increases in revenue are covered, as are reduced costs and improved efficiency. However, remember that you will be competing in an environment that may seem less personal than the one in which you have traditionally participated. You will need to ensure that any solution you commission is able to provide rich interactions between your company and your customers. B2B e-commerce is moving beyond simple buying and selling—it is also about collaborating with trading partners for mutual benefit. In addition to providing your product information and a means of purchasing, you should also consider how customized products are presented and how presales and postsales support is provided. Additionally, you should determine how you can communicate effectively with your trading partners in ways other than those involved in the exchange of data for the selling process. In short, you will require collaborative mechanisms, of one sort or another, from your B2B e-commerce solution.

Off-the-shelf sell-side solutions vary quite considerably in the collaborative mechanisms they offer. To realize the business objective of collaborating effectively with your trading partners, you will need to assess these mechanisms carefully. If none of the off-the-shelf solutions provides adequate mechanisms, you will need to investigate the possibilities for extending these solutions or even building a custom mechanism for this key business objective. *Chapter 4, "Business Strategies and Solutions,"* discusses the pros and cons of extending solutions, as well as building custom ones, in more depth.

Any system that you commission *must* provide you with a mechanism for differentiating your products and services from those of your competitors. There are many different mechanisms that allow this differentiation. Because this is a fundamental objective of most suppliers, it will be a key theme throughout the rest of this book. We will talk more about how you can realize this key empowerment objective in Chapters 3, 4, and 5.

The solution you choose must also allow you to improve your market agility by allowing you to sell through multiple sales channels from the same solution. If you need to exploit a new channel or change how you participate in an existing one, you will not want to have to wait months, weeks, or even days to implement your new business strategy. Additionally, you will not want such changes to incur significant costs to your IT department. We delve further into this issue in *Chapter 3, "Technology as a Strategic Weapon for Suppliers," and Chapter 6, "Managing the Future: Buyers, Suppliers, and B2B E-Commerce."*

Managing Your Online Business

One of the important objectives that you will have identified is being able to integrate with your existing line of business applications. A key requirement for your B2B e-commerce solution is smooth and seamless operation with other systems that you may use, such as SCM and financial systems.

Being able to analyze the vast amounts of data that online selling can generate in an efficient, timely, and useful manner is also a critical area of functionality that you will want to make sure your B2B e-commerce solution delivers. After all, your future business strategies depend on the analysis of all kinds of business data, in this, the Information Age. Many sell-side solutions include analysis features of some sort, so you will be able to realize the business objective of making well-founded decisions. However, you will need to investigate this critical area of functionality on a *per-solution* basis.

Summary: Supplier Empowerment

We have identified some fantastic opportunities to achieve goals such as reducing costs, increasing revenue, and improving efficiency. If you understand all of the opportunities that are available to you, and you are aware of all the pitfalls, you should be able to put together a strategy that will allow you to do much more than reach the targets for cost reduction and increased revenue that you had in the past. You will be able to easily *surpass* those targets and position your company for the future.

Selling your goods and services online means that you are moving into a new business environment. As you do so, you must continue to exercise control over your selling processes, even though parts of them will be automated. You must continue working toward objectives such as increasing revenues, reducing costs, improving competitive differentiation, reducing errors, and making better decisions. We discuss matching solutions to requirements in more detail later in this book.

Technology as a Strategic Weapon for Suppliers

Suppliers exist in many different shapes and sizes. Millions of organizations provide goods and services to trading partners and other customers. As business-to-business (B2B) e-commerce becomes more established, your company, as a supplier organization, will share similar goals and concerns with other suppliers. All will be faced with exciting new prospects for improving their business, and all will face technological challenges that must be overcome to exploit those opportunities.

Sometimes, the degree of similarity between different businesses tends to be obscured by the disparate characteristics of those companies and how they actually function. For example, if you manage a single-site manufacturing business that supplies nuts and bolts to the rail industry, you could be forgiven for concluding that you have very little in common with a Fortune 500 corporation that provides financial services to a long list of blue-chip clients. If you run a small business supplying stationery to local companies, you might not think that you share similar challenges and goals with a global supplier of computer hardware.

Whether you are a multinational corporation or a single-product trader, whether you sell to thousands of business customers or have a handful of trading partners, whether you have an existing, complex IT infrastructure with a large IT department or you outsource all of your technology requirements to IT specialists, you can be sure of one thing in today's business environment—you can use technology as a strategic weapon for improving your business and increasing your market agility.

In this chapter, we will show you that all suppliers can benefit from the use of technology, regardless of their size and complexity. However, you need to be aware that not all technology strategies are appropriate for all organizations. Just as the different characteristics of each company demand that it uses different business strategies in the pursuit of its goals, each company's use of technology as a strategic weapon will also differ. What might be a good technical solution for one organization might be of little use for another. Investments in technology that can be quickly amortized by improved returns for one company might not be a wise investment for another, especially if the increase in revenue is not large enough (or does not materialize quickly enough) to offset the cost of the solution.

In this chapter, we examine the supplier landscape and how technology can affect it. We provide ideas about the level of automation that can be applied to business processes, and discuss how these concepts influence the way in which you communicate with customers, trading partners, and your own employees. We describe how to use technology as a strategic weapon that your company can use to achieve its goals, specifically from the perspective of supplier organizations and how they sell to business customers. We conclude this chapter with an outline of an economic justification framework that you can use to assess the benefits you will gain from the appropriate use of technology against the costs you will incur.

Supplier Landscape

Consider this scenario: You are a key business decision maker for your organization, which supplies goods and services to other businesses. You are responsible for the strategy of your company. The future viability of the business lives or dies based on the decisions you make. Your company, like virtually all other companies, needs to reduce costs, increase revenue, empower its employees, increase its market agility, and grow in an increasingly competitive environment. Your company is founded on excellent business principles, such as outstanding customer service, admirable employee relations, and the exceptionally high-quality goods and services that provide the backbone of your offerings. In short, your company considers itself to be the best value player in your given market.

Rather than simply sitting back and watching your company grow, you still have many concerns. You are aware that you can fare even better than you have in recent times. You are sure that you can reduce business costs *and* increase revenues. You feel that the employees at your company can be more productive *and* happier in their work as well. You can see advantages in being able to adjust more quickly to market conditions, such as being able to attract a wider range of customers with more responsive offerings. The question is, *How can you achieve all of this?*

The answer is simple, yet by no means simplistic—you can use technology to improve your business processes. Automated systems can allow your employees to work more efficiently *and* bestow a feeling of true empower-ment. A strong, rich, Web presence can strengthen your brands. Being able to accept orders electronically over the Internet can streamline the processes that buyers must undertake as they purchase your goods and services, making your company more attractive as a supplier. Additionally, these buyers can be exposed to the full value proposition of your goods and services as they step through the procurement process. You can implement these automated systems in such a way that you are able to modify your offerings much more quickly than ever before. You can have good decision-support systems that allow you to analyze your business data in a truly useful manner. You can use this analysis to make quick, well-founded decisions, such as how and when to tap into new revenue streams, how to maximize returns from successful areas of your business, and how to improve underperforming areas.

Why Automate?

After you have appreciated all of the opportunities that are available for improving your business as a supplier, you clearly see the decision you have to make. Do you use technology as a strategic weapon to improve your business, or do you look at more traditional approaches, such as those you have used in the past? Hopefully, the answer to this question is clear. You need to incorporate the use of technology as part of your business strategy.

Note   We are not advocating that the use of technology dominates all of your well-founded business principles. Far from it—we understand only too well that your traditional strategies have been key in getting your company to where it is now. We *are* suggesting, however, that you need to consider the use of technology alongside your traditional business considerations as a potent force that needs to be harnessed to work *for* your company in this, the Information Age.

You thus make the decision to use technology as a strategic weapon that will allow you to continue to compete more effectively within your market. You are convinced that you can achieve the much sought-after benefits for which you have always been striving, such as increased revenue, lower costs, and so on. You are also content that the appropriate use of technology will give your company an enhanced agility that will allow you to maintain a high quality of service to your customers, also allowing your business to take advantage of volatile market conditions and trends in a timely manner. You are satisfied that you will have a useful decision-support system in place to allow you to do just that, as well as to gain more insight into your business than previously possible.

What to Automate?

Having concluded that using technology as part of your business strategy will enable you to compete effectively in your market, you may be tempted to turn the issue of what needs to be achieved over to the IT management team at your organization. Alternatively, you might decide to outsource your newly recognized IT requirements to a solution provider. The danger in jumping to this type of action at this stage is that there are many standard solutions and technologies available. Some of these might be just what your company requires, whereas others could be wholly inappropriate for your business needs. There are also likely to be business issues that are unique to your company for which no standard solutions exist.

We don't wish to cast aspersions on your IT staff (or your solution providers), but you should realize that many technology specialists will not have a good understanding of your company's business requirements. Correctly aligning a technical solution with business needs is always a challenge (more on that later in this chapter). New technologies appear at an ever-increasing rate these days, and IT specialists are often tempted to use products in which they are interested, or those that appear to be at the cutting edge of the IT industry, merely for the sake of the technology itself. Whether a given technology or solution *should* be used, based on a thorough analysis of the business benefits it will bring, is not always at the top of the agenda for the people who will deliver your solution. The danger, then, is that your decision to use technology as a strategic weapon to achieve your business goals can easily turn against you. *An inappropriate solution can sometimes be worse than a failure to use technology as a key part of your business strategy—it may become just another overall cost to your company.*

The question that now needs answering is, *Which parts of our business process can benefit from automated solutions?* The response to this question must be tempered with a consideration of the costs that will be incurred to achieve the automated solution, the time frame required for a successful implementation, and the ease of integration with your existing IT infrastructure. An analysis of the costs should include an estimate of the total cost of ownership (TCO) for the solution after it has been deployed, such as the amount of administration it will require. What you should look for is an over-all solution that is a true business benefit to your company. The initial costs need to be regained quickly, and the time frame for implementation should be appropriate to allow you to integrate with the new business models that are emerging. The TCO should not be prohibitive and, just as important, the over-all solution needs to be flexible enough to adapt in the face of future changes and trends in the practice of online selling.

Like all other commercial entities, your business depends on your inter-action with customers. You will also have contact with other businesses that you perceive as trading partners. You and your business partners often derive mutual benefit from working closely together to achieve shared goals. You will almost certainly be in a supply chain of one sort or another, where you, too, have suppliers of your own. Finally, you depend on an efficient workforce and knowledgeable employees to run your business on a day-to-day basis. Your business processes, then, have many facets and different types of interac-tion. Taking a holistic view of your business is key when making the decision about what to automate to achieve your business goals. The next step you have to take, then, is to analyze which parts of your business and which partic-ular business processes can be automated to provide the most significant positive impact.

Customer Interactions

One of the key interactions for any business is providing goods and services to customers, but you knew that already. The approach to business-to-consumer (B2C) e-commerce has matured significantly over the last few years. Back in the earlier stages of the Internet revolution, there seemed to be an over-whelming rush to get a Web presence, and understandably so. As it was then, the new media provided by the World Wide Web offered an extremely low-cost option for advertising goods and services with an emphasis on reaching new customers in far-flung places.

The next step was to start actively selling over the Web. This involved pub-lishing catalogs of products and services and allowing customers to place orders online and even pay for purchases using credit cards. The ability to sell products 24 hours a day, 7 days a week had a significant impact on many busi-nesses. No longer were they restricted to trading during traditional business hours in their particular time zones.

Undoubtedly, using the Web for all of these goals has elements of good business sense. However, successful selling using the Web should do more than simply advertise your existence and should go *further* than merely providing a mechanism for purchasing goods and services. It should also be used as a means of actively retaining existing customers. You can achieve this by providing not only catalogs of your offerings on the Web, but also online support and postsales services. In a nutshell, your Web presence can be used to *communicate,* and more importantly, *collaborate* with your customers. This can benefit your clients by allowing you to add your own unique value to the purchasing process, so you can retain your enviable record of quality of service. It also opens up the possibility for you to sell related goods and services to those customers, which is often known as *cross-sell*. Additionally, you can implement the practice known as *up-sell,* whereby you promote the existence of higher valued alternatives to those products that your customers have traditionally purchased. Finally, data collected from the transactions serviced by your Web site can provide an invaluable source of insight when you analyze your company's performance as part of your ongoing strategy. This is an important way for your customers to communicate with you.

You need to consider all of these issues when deciding whether to (and how to) automate interactions with your customers.

Trading Partner Interactions

Although companies have exchanged data electronically for years now, the use of the Internet and the World Wide Web to communicate with trading partners is a less mature idea than the B2C interactions described previously. However, the interactions with your trading partners through B2B e-commerce solutions have certain facets in common with B2C interactions.

B2B e-commerce is primarily concerned with streamlining the business processes undertaken by your company and its trading partners. This involves exchanging business data, such as purchase orders and invoices, electronically. The efficiency gains that both you and your trading partners can make from this basic concept are considerable.

B2B e-commerce solutions are geared toward the direct trading of goods and services between organizations. These solutions have some similarities with B2C e-commerce applications, because a buyer is purchasing goods from you, the supplier. However, the two types of solutions usually differ in a number of ways. These differences include the following:

- **Type of customer.** B2C solutions are geared toward selling to end consumers, although business customers often make purchases from such solutions. B2B solutions, as the name implies, are geared toward servicing the needs of business customers, which are often different and, perhaps, more complex.

- **Level of human interaction.** B2C solutions are invariably designed to provide purchasing mechanisms that directly engage the person buying the products. Consumers typically read information in a Web browser, choose products, check out their order, supply details of the delivery address that should be used, and provide some means of payment (usually credit card). B2B solutions vary in the amount of human interaction required. At one end of the scale, details such as delivery addresses, payment mechanisms, and so on, are exchanged automatically, even if an employee is actually browsing product catalogs. At the other end of the scale, an intelligent procurement application may be placing orders in response to low stock levels in the purchaser's inventory system, with no human interaction required at all.

- **Methods of payment.** As described already, B2C solutions usually include the use of credit cards as the means of settlement. Although B2B solutions can include this payment mechanism, it is more common to exchange purchase orders and invoices electronically as part of the buying and selling process.

- **Contractual issues.** Consumers are not usually restricted in what they can buy from a B2C Web site. Business purchases, however, are sometimes subject to contract. Preferred rates may have been negotiated between trading partners, based on sales volume, total spending, or other appropriate metrics; discounts may be applied in some cases but not others; and some value-added services will be negotiated between certain trading partners but will not apply across the board.

- **Collaboration.** Purchases made by consumers are usually considered a singular event. Certainly, it may be desirable to use information about previous purchases made by consumers to tailor their view of your B2C Web site the next time that they visit, such as providing advertising that targets goods and services in which you know these particular consumers are interested. It is not usually feasible, however, to build collaborative relationships with consumers. In contrast, it *is* possible to collaborate with your trading partners—both you, as the supplier, and the buyer organization can benefit from rich, strong relationships that are centered around the process of buying and selling goods and services.

Employee Interactions

Because your employees are critical to the success of your business, you need to consider the strategic benefits that the appropriate use of technology can bring to them. Any change in the way you do business with either customers or trading partners, brought about by automating certain processes, will inevitably affect the way your staff members carry out their day-to-day work. For example, automated B2C solutions affect how your employees interact with consumers, and automated B2B solutions influence how they interact with your trading partners. However, the issue of automating certain aspects of your employees' work is more pervasive than that. For example, you will obviously be concerned with removing inefficiencies in the processes used by your employees in dealing with trading partners, but you should also be concerned with doing the same for how they file expense claims, book meeting rooms, fill in their time sheets, and so on. That is, you should determine if processes not directly connected to trading partners or customers can be improved by the use of technology.

This issue is perhaps more complex than it first appears. You will need to consider numerous factors, such as how new systems will integrate with existing ones already in use by your employees. In fact, this is also a consideration for the B2C and B2B areas of your business. These must also integrate with other systems, as we described in *Chapter 2, "Business-to-Business E-Commerce Objectives for Suppliers."*

You will also need to assess training costs for your employees and perform exercises such as user-acceptance testing of new solutions. An often hidden cost is the possibility that employee efficiency may experience an initial downturn as your staff acquaint themselves with new technology and new solutions.

Another aim for automating the interactions with your employees is the concept of employee empowerment. All employees can benefit from timely access to relevant information, and allowing easy access to relevant data when it is needed makes for a more knowledgeable workforce, not just a more efficient one. Empowering your employees requires your company to organize useful information into a suitable structure and make this information available when employees need it. You will find that having knowledgeable, empowered employees is in itself a strategic weapon that you can use to improve how you sell to your business customers, among the many other functions of your business.

In summary, you need to think about all areas of your business, including how you interact with customers, trading partners, and employees, when you are making the decision about what business processes you want to automate and what level of automation you require.

Technological Challenges

You have now identified what needs to be automated to benefit your business at this particular time. Before you can pass this information to the IT department (or solution provider), your last challenge is to commission a solution that meets your business needs. Therein lies your problem. Your requirements for the solution, like your business processes, are unique to your company. There are already software vendors who may offer solutions to part (or all) of your requirements. The scope and functionality of these solutions vary widely at present, and the rapid emergence of vendors in this market serves only to exacerbate the variability of what is available. Add in the wide variations in price for different solutions, as well as issues such as the extensibility of the software and whether the functionality can evolve alongside your existing business processes and technology investments, and you are left with an often bewildering choice.

Limited Functionality of Most Solutions

Many solutions are limited in one way or another. Not all solutions that purport to enable suppliers to compete in the current business environment contain all of the functionality that you require. Some solutions are suitable only for the largest and most complicated enterprises, and the costs associated with these solutions may well be prohibitive, especially if you are a small or medium-sized supplier. Further, some solutions are vertically aligned, targeting only specific industries.

We have compiled a list of supplier-enablement solution characteristics, gathered by analyzing the offerings from a number of software vendors. Before we describe each characteristic, it is important that you understand that a single solution, offering all of the characteristics we describe, is a rare thing. Most solutions only offer a subset of this functionality.

Also, bear in mind that, even as we write this book, the B2B e-commerce market is changing and evolving, not only in technological terms but also in the appearance of new business models and the disappearance of others. However, as we are not writing about any one specific technology or any specific business model, the guidance provided in these chapters should remain appropriate long after this book is published.

Sell-Side Functionality

Sell-side functionality is the general ability to make your products and services available to customers in rich, collaborative ways. For the supplier, this can include selling both to consumers through Web sites and to business customers through their procurement applications. It may also include selling to business customers through public or private electronic marketplaces. Typical solutions involve all facets of an effective Web site, along with the ability to make your company's goods and services available by producing and publishing catalogs that can be used in automated procurement systems and marketplaces. They typically include mechanisms whereby business customers (or the general public) can purchase your goods and services in an automated manner.

You may be surprised that not all vendors provide sell-side functionality as part of their solutions. Where this functionality is not provided, you will be expected to implement your own sell-side features, either from scratch or by integrating solutions from several different vendors.

Remember, as we have already discussed in this chapter (and in other sections of this book), the use of technology to sell your goods and services will ideally go a lot further than simply providing catalogs and purchasing mechanisms. You will almost certainly want to use the sell-side features of any solution to form the basis of real, useful communication and collaboration with your customers and trading partners. You will, therefore, want to investigate whether a particular sell-side solution actually delivers these additional facilities.

Front-End Integration

We introduced the concept of electronic procurement applications and marketplaces in *Chapter 1, "The Role of Suppliers in Business-to-Business E-Commerce."* The ability to communicate with a variety of these applications or selling channels is known as *front-end integration*. You should be aware of the following:

- There is an ever-increasing number of procurement applications appearing in the market as you read this book.

- All customers implement electronic procurement differently, even if they use applications from the same procurement software vendor.

- Private marketplaces also exist and are maintained by large organizations solely for the use of their approved trading partners.

- Some marketplaces are vertically aligned, whereas others offer more general opportunities for selling goods and services.

Given all of that, you will not be surprised to learn that a wide variation exists in the front-end integration needs of suppliers. You will need to investigate the front-end capabilities of any solution very closely to determine whether it provides integration with the marketplaces and procurement applications with which you wish to operate. Bear in mind that, as discussed in *Chapter 1, "The Role of Suppliers in Business-to-Business E-Commerce,"* integrating with some procurement systems and marketplaces can offer a poor value proposition for suppliers, whereas others operate on a more equitable basis.

Back-End Integration

Back-end integration refers to the ability of a solution to communicate and exchange data with other systems that you may use in your company. Some questions that you might need to ask about a solution (depending on your current systems) include the following:

- Can it integrate with your accounting and/or enterprise resource planning (ERP) systems to leverage product information, inventory, and order management capabilities?

- Can it integrate with your customer relationship management (CRM) systems to utilize and contribute to the data about your customers?

- Can it integrate with your supply-chain management (SCM) systems to produce and consume supply chain information such as inventory levels and demand forecasting information?

- Can it integrate with your decision-support systems to maintain and improve the way you analyze your business performance?

By using the word *integrate* in the preceding questions, we really mean that the different systems communicate with each other so that the B2B e-commerce solution benefits from data in the other systems, but also that those other systems benefit from the data generated by the B2B solution. As with the front-end characteristics, you will want to closely examine the back-end integration capabilities of any solution.

Remote Shopping

We have already discussed at length in previous chapters the issue of avoiding commoditization and the necessity of differentiating your company and its goods and services from those of your competitors. Because this is an extremely important issue, we will reiterate that you do not want to compete on price alone in the B2B e-commerce world. Publishing a brief product description along with its price and item number is not enough. You did not compete on such a basis prior to the Internet revolution, and there is no reason for doing so now, as you embrace B2B e-commerce. You may produce high-quality goods and provide the best services available in your sector, so you can justifiably charge a premium for your offerings. The last thing you will want to achieve from your B2B e-commerce initiative is to have buyers (or their automated procurement systems) judge your products and services against those of your competitors on price alone, especially if those competitors offer cheaper but lower quality versions of your goods and services.

Instead, imagine that an employee of one of your customers is using that organization's procurement application. She needs to order a new projector for the marketing department. She views high-level descriptions of projectors from various suppliers, one of which is your company. The employee clicks the photograph of one of your models, and the next thing she sees is information that fully describes the features and benefits of this particular projector. She is also presented with a range of options that allow her to configure the projector to the company's exact specification, such as type of power supply, type of bulb, and so on. Additionally, she has the ability to order extra bulbs, and even the latest style of projection board with your patented no-glare finish. On top of all that, the employee is exposed to supplementary information about the post-sales support that you offer, and she can see details of the guarantees that both you and the projector manufacturer supply. All the time that she is viewing this valuable information, she is secure in the knowledge that she is still operating within the confines of her company's business rules. For example, she knows that the purchases she is making will remain within budget, or else she will be notified at this early stage. She also knows that contractual details, such as preferred supplier rates and extra service agreements made between you, the supplier, and her organization will be honored. This means that when she has completed the purchasing process, the order will be seamlessly placed in the company's ordering system.

We term this functionality *remote shopping,* although it is referred to by many other names by various procurement application vendors. In short, remote shopping is the process whereby an electronic procurement application or a marketplace browsing session can collaborate with your sell-side features to allow you to expose your own unique value to the purchasing process. It allows you to differentiate your goods and services from those of your competitors, and helps you to avoid commoditization, in which you would be forced to compete on price alone. Additionally, remote shopping features allow you, the supplier, to maintain the catalogs used by the buyer. You can keep product details (such as price, description, and other valuable information) up to date, you can add new products to the catalog if you want to sell new items, and you can remove discontinued products from those catalogs, all in real time. In effect, buyers access your catalog from their procurement application, but the catalog information is actually retrieved over the Internet from *your* solution. One advantage of this approach is simply that your business customers will not have to import updated catalogs into their systems every time pricing or other information changes. Perhaps more important, you can be assured that your business customers have access to your latest product details and additional value-added information, allowing you to remain in control of what you sell and how you sell it.

Not all solutions offer the same level of remote shopping functionality. In fact, the types of remote shopping supported are largely determined by the functionality provided by the purchasing applications used by your customers. Some solutions offer a comprehensive list of supported remote shopping standards and allow easy integration with many automated procurement and marketplace applications. Others have limited or no support for these capabilities and will require significant work by the implementers of the solution if you require this critical functionality.

Solution Targets

One last solution characteristic that we have identified is the type of supplier to which the vendors are aiming their solutions. Although this is not really a functionality issue, it is important nevertheless. Most solutions have a "sweet spot," whereby the standard functionality performs optimally within a particular range of capacity. Using a particular solution outside of its targeted range of capacity will sometimes lead to poor performance, which may demand additional configuration or development work to remedy.

At present, most (but not all) solutions are aimed at large enterprises or medium-to-large companies, and the costs associated with these solutions are often very high. Some are really aimed at only the largest and most complex suppliers. If your company is small, or even medium-sized, you will want to identify solutions that are appropriate to your scale of operation. This is not just a case of finding a solution within what may be a limited budget, but it also involves issues such as operating costs and administrative needs of the solution.

Technology as a Strategic Weapon

Amid the issues identified so far in this chapter, such as deciding what to automate and finding appropriate solutions for your needs, there is an opportunity you might like to consider. Rather than merely using technology to keep abreast of your competitors by achieving the traditional business goals of reducing costs, improving efficiency, and so on, you can use technology to sell more effectively and instigate a revolution in the way you interact with your business customers. We are well aware that many marketing campaigns, advertising materials, and other types of promotion use the word *revolution* ad nauseam. So overused is that particular term that, as consumers, we do not even bat an eye when we are informed about the newest, revolutionary hair-care product. None of the authors of this book, for example, has ever experienced a shampoo that made us change the way we wash our hair. So, it is not without careful thought that we propose you *can* use technology in today's environment to revolutionize the way in which you interact with and sell to your business customers. In short, you can even the power balance between buyers and your company as a supplier.

Empowering Suppliers

Traditionally, the customer has always been right. Actually, we can all think of situations that clearly refute this ideology, but the gist of this oft-repeated mantra is that the direction of monetary flow is all-important in a business relationship. As important as receiving money from customers may be (it is the reason you are in business, after all), you may consider the subjugation of all other matters to this one a little crude. We certainly do. Consumers of your goods and services are now looking to you to provide more than just a wrapped product. They are looking for all sorts of other things, such as advice on how best to use your offerings, friendly and helpful postsales support, and so on. In a nutshell, they are looking to communicate and collaborate more with you, the supplier. In turn, you are beginning to look for more than just a monetary return on your products.

You, too, can benefit from communication with your customers, including feedback about how they use your current products, what the good things and the bad things are about your relationship with them, and information about how you can cooperate in the future for mutual benefit. In short, you have a relationship with your customers in which the exchange of goods and services, along with the flow of money, is only one of the important exchanges, a relationship in which collaboration and the flow of information in both directions is crucial to both your success and that of your customers. You can now view the balance of power as exactly that—a balance. Ideally, you can formulate a business strategy in which your trading partners depend on the value that you supply to them as much as you depend on the money that they pay to you. Rather than merely using technology to improve your business in traditional ways, you can use it as a strategic weapon to bring about that balance of power.

The Supplier's Perspective

Much emphasis in recent times has been given to the buyer's perspective of B2B e-commerce. This is not surprising, because the value proposition for buyers who automate their purchasing systems is clear and well documented (check back to the MS Market example in Chapter 1, *"The Role of Suppliers in Business-to-Business E-Commerce,"* if you are not convinced of the benefits that can be achieved by buyers when they streamline and automate their procurement processes). Given that the buyer's perspective is well known and the value proposition of trading online for suppliers is unclear, we would like to set the record straight. You can strategically place your company at the center of the various business transactions in which you are involved by using technology to integrate with your various sales channels to provide a unified base for a multifaceted selling operation. Figure 3-1 illustrates this concept.

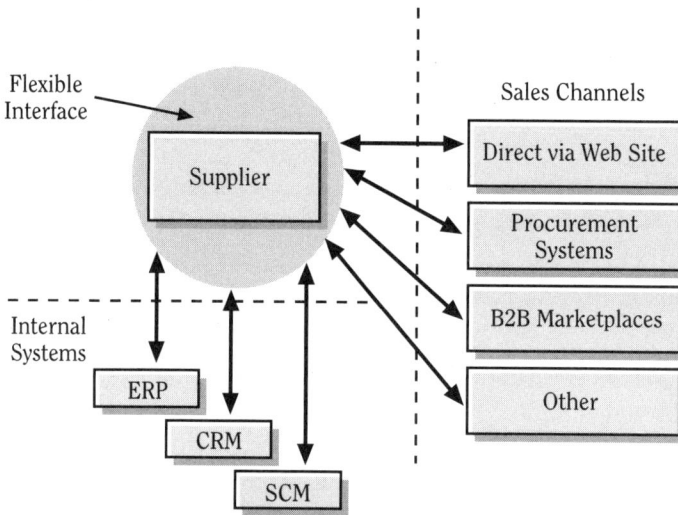

Figure 3-1.   *A unified base for the supplier's perspective.*

As long as you can compete within these channels on more than price alone, and as long as you can build the type of relationships with your various partners that make your company indispensable to their organizations, you will quickly be seen as a pivotal player in your particular market.

Differentiating Your Offerings

It is worth reiterating at this point that the key to your success in any sales channel is differentiating your goods and services from those of your competitors. Almost certainly, you will not want to compete on price alone. If the solution you choose allows only that, we can safely predict that the use of technology will cease to be a strategic weapon unless it is your company's goal to compete primarily on price. It is important that any solution you choose allows you to communicate your true value as a supplier to all of your customers and across *all* of your sales channels to be truly effective.

Supplier Agility

The strategic placement of your business at the center of your multiple sales channels relies on your ability to commission a system that does not need reinventing every time you need to tap into a new source of revenue or when you need to work in a new business environment. Remember that earlier in this chapter we said our guidance in empowering suppliers would survive changes in business models as well as changes in technology? Well, this is how. It is vitally important that any solution you choose can adapt so that new trading partners, and even new business paradigms, can be simply plugged into your base solution with minimal effort. In fact, that is a good way of looking at this issue. New partners need to plug into your solution, but they may require a differently shaped socket than those with which you currently work. If the base solution is adaptable, your IT providers will simply have to design the plug and socket interface to allow collaboration and trading to commence. Undoubtedly, as new trading partners collaborate with you, and as the way of doing business electronically over the Internet evolves, new sockets will have to be developed, but what you will really want to avoid is going through the whole process of architecting a complete solution again. In short, the solution must be capable of evolving as quickly as you develop your business. We provide advice about building solutions that can evolve alongside your business strategies in *Chapter 6, "Managing the Future: Buyers, Suppliers, and B2B E-Commerce."*

Economic Justification for Your Decisions: A Framework

In *Chapter 4, "Business Strategies and Solutions,"* we will delve into details about what attributes to look for in a solution. For now, we tackle the often thorny issue of financially aligning any solution you may commission with the other business strategies of your organization. Assuming that *you* are convinced of the need to use technology not just as a reactive, short-term, tactical tool but as a planned, long-term, strategic weapon for your business, you will need to justify any initiative in financial terms. Depending on your organizational structure and where you fit into that scheme, you may need to justify your proposals in different terms. For example, you might need to address the concerns of your IT managers regarding operating costs that their department will incur, and you might need to convince the chief financial officer (CFO) of the return on investment (ROI) that you expect. You might need to advise the chief executive officer (CEO) about how the solution will increase revenue, and you might need to illustrate to the chief operating officer (COO) the increase in efficiency and the reduction in business costs that will accrue for the company.

As important as identifying who in your company needs to be convinced of these opportunities and their related benefits is the need to present the case in terms that the particular stakeholder will understand. You should, wherever possible, use metrics that the stakeholder already applies to other business strategies. For example, the CFO will readily understand your case if it is supported by metrics, such as the net present value (NPV) of your investment, if he or she uses that method to assess ROI in other areas of the business.

Note   NPV is just one standard calculation. It is the balance of cash, determined by subtracting the cost of an investment from the income that the investment will generate, taking into account that payments will be spread and income received over periods in the future. The calculation therefore involves a consideration of the rate of inflation so that the balance can be viewed in today's terms. Your CFO might well use different metrics.

If you run a small operation, you may have fewer stakeholders with whom you need to communicate. However, even if you are the sole decision maker in your company, you should still put together a robust economic justification for your initiative. This exercise allows you to quantify the advantages and disadvantages of the different types of solutions we describe in *Chapter 4, "Business Strategies and Solutions,"* and *Chapter 5, "Implementing a Solution,"* against your own unique circumstances. It will allow you to do the same for different solutions that will undoubtedly evolve in the future.

Over the next few pages, we outline a framework that you can use to build a business case for justifying the use of technology as a key part of your sales and marketing strategy. The framework has a general nature, but we provide issues and examples that are specific to supplier organizations as we discuss each part.

Note   The framework that we discuss is loosely based on part of a complete strategy that Microsoft uses both internally and with their clients. The strategy is called the Microsoft REJ Framework. REJ stands for Rapid Economic Justification. The framework was developed in conjunction with key business schools, industry analysts, and Microsoft's partners and customers. You can find more information about the Microsoft REJ Framework by visiting *http:// www.microsoft.com/value* or by searching for REJ at Microsoft's Web site: *http://www.microsoft.com*. In addition, you can read an entire case study about the Microsoft REJ Framework and supplier empowerment in Appendix A of this book.

Background Issues

Before we jump straight into the framework, it will be useful to consider some background issues.

To provide a coherent argument to support your technology initiatives, you must understand that key personnel in modern companies are looking to quantify the benefits of IT to their business. We are not just talking about an assessment of the reduced TCO that IT managers may reap from one solution or another. Rather, we are thinking of the impact that IT investments have in relation to other strategic investments traditionally undertaken in most companies, such as marketing, research and development, sales initiatives, and so on. To put it simply, your CFO needs to be convinced that spending money on your IT initiative is a better investment than channeling that same money into a new marketing campaign or an expansion of research and development.

One challenge you will need to tackle is quantifying the benefits of your strategy in traditional economic terms. The problem with which you will be faced is that traditional accounting methods do not easily lend themselves to quantifying the absolute value of IT investments. Further, such methods are geared toward assessing the ROI for other key areas of the business, such as sales initiatives, research and development, and marketing. Already, you are competing on an uneven playing field. You will realize that you are definitely up against it when you find that quantifying the *costs* associated with IT solutions is well understood by the CFO and CEO!

At this point we should make something clear: models and techniques do exist for justifying strategic investment in IT. These models have evolved to a state in which they offer extremely good mathematical certainty and precision. However, they require that vast amounts of data be collected, and consequently take a significant amount of time to prepare. You may have heard of the phrase *Internet-time*. The connotation behind this term is that technology *and* business models now evolve at an often alarming rate. If you spend too much time analyzing how to exploit a certain business model or technology, by the time you are ready to take advantage of your investment, the world has moved on and you are left with a relic of days gone by. You also may have heard of the term *analysis paralysis*—this is exactly what people are talking about when they use that term.

As accurate as they are, models that require a heavy investment in time will be of little help to you in taking advantage of the Internet to improve your position as a supplier. What you need to do is put together your justification in a very short time, while maintaining credibility. We now introduce a framework that you can use to rapidly prepare your business case. The general steps that you should consider taking as you work toward a justification are as follows:

1. Assess your business.
2. Define your solution requirements.
3. Estimate benefits and costs.
4. Identify risks.
5. Assemble your findings.

Assessing Your Business

Aligning your IT-based initiative with the other business strategies of your company is key to your success in being able to justify any investment in technology. Appropriate alignment will enable the whole exercise to proceed quickly, allowing you to focus on only those issues that are important to your particular business. In addition, you will be able to identify proper business goals for your initiative that are consistent with the objectives of other key stakeholders in your organization.

Although the manner in which you approach this crucial stage should be appropriate to your company, you might consider interviewing the other key stakeholders in your business to gain insight into their general aims, at the very least.

You may decide to formalize this step to include definitions of what your colleagues see as critical success factors (CSFs). You should strive to understand these factors from the perspective of the particular stakeholder. For example, the CEO might well consider increased profit as critical to the success of any business initiative, whereas the COO might consider a slightly narrower factor, such as a reduction in costs, as the primary concern.

You may even go a step further and define how each stakeholder typically measures the success of his or her CSFs. For example, you might determine that the CEO measures increased profit by an upturn in earnings per share (EPS). The COO might measure operational efficiency as revenue per unit of output divided by employee cost per unit of output. Such metrics are often termed *key performance indicators* (KPIs).

It will not take you too much time to build a matrix of stakeholders and their CSFs and KPIs. An example of such a matrix is shown in Table 3-1.

Table 3-1.   An Example CFS/KPI Matrix

Stakeholder	CSF	KPI
CEO	Increased revenue and profit	EPS
CFO	Large or rapid ROI	NPV
COO	Increased operational efficiency	Revenue per unit of output/ employee cost per unit of output

Once you have gathered this information from the stakeholders, you should analyze the activities in your company that affect the CSFs, either positively or negatively. For example, you might determine that your employees currently spend a lot of time filling in paper-based forms when dealing with orders, and this negatively affects efficiency. You may find that your staff members struggle to keep up with current demand, which is obviously a good sign from the perspective of market conditions, but it needs exploiting to realize even more benefit. In addition, this demand needs managing to keep your workforce happy.

You should analyze these types of activities thoroughly in the context of how your IT initiative can be effectively applied to each key area.

Defining the Solution

Let's say that you have identified the following negative impact: *Sales staff members spend a significant amount of time filling in paper-based forms when dealing with orders. This prevents them from spending enough time actively selling goods and services.* You can align your solution with this important business issue by defining a value statement, such as this: *By automating the sales process, we can increase the amount of time that employees spend actively selling to customers.*

You should define your complete IT-based strategy in these simple terms. Rather than spending too much time creating reams of content about how your solution addresses the needs of the business, you can again construct a simple matrix that enables the other key stakeholders at your company to see at a glance how your solution aligns with their business issues. The matrix should include the following information:

- The activity in question

- The current state of affairs

- The desired state

- How the state can be achieved (referred to as an *enabler*)

- Your value statement for this activity

A useful solution matrix might look something like Table 3-2.

Table 3-2. An Example Solution Matrix

Activity	Current State	Desired State	Enabler	Value Statement
Processing orders	Staff spend too much time filling in paper-based forms; High rate of errors in order entry and processing; Only able to process orders when staff is available	Efficient entry of order details; Low error rate; 24/7 access for customers	Web-based electronic order entry system that complements the efforts of the sales staff	By automating the sales process, we can increase the amount of time that employees spend actively selling to customers, reduce dedicated order entry staff and associated errors, and receive orders in real time, 24 hours a day.
Dealing with customer demand	We lose some sales by failing to respond to customers	Ability to capture all sales	Self-service order system for our customers	By allowing orders to be placed electronically by our customers, we can increase sales revenue.

At the end of this step, you might want to check the value statements with the key stakeholders so that you are sure the statements are well aligned with your business goals. After that, you can commence with your cost–benefit analysis.

Estimating Costs and Benefits

You can look at the balance of cost versus benefit in a number of ways. You might consider an increase in revenue and profits brought about by your investment as the crucial factor, or you might view the return as how much money can be saved by the investment. Commercial organizations typically use some variation of the wealth-generating approach, rather than the cost-saving method. (Incidentally, nonprofit organizations more commonly use the latter approach.) To successfully estimate the cost–benefit balance that your initiative can bring about, you will need a clear understanding of the cash flows associated with your proposals. Bear in mind that a good B2B e-commerce solution should both increase revenues *and* decrease costs.

An estimation of the cost of an IT-based solution is generally straightforward and simply requires diligence on your part in ensuring that you identify all costs. You may find estimating the benefits, however, a more daunting prospect. Traditionally, the benefits provided by investment in IT have been measured by reduction in labor costs. We have already discussed that the strategic use of technology can go much further than this.

In some cases, the calculation will actually be straightforward. For example, imagine that you employ 60 salespeople, and pay them an average salary of $40,000 per year (including benefits, commission, and so on). Now, you estimate that the automated order entry system will increase the productivity of your sales staff so that they can make 33 percent more sales by using their time more efficiently. This equates to recruiting 20 more staff members into your current sales system. You could calculate the benefit, then, as the salary for the 20 extra staff members ($800,000).

In other cases, the problem is more difficult; for example, how can you put a hard-cash figure against the benefits of being able to analyze data obtained by collaborating with your business partners? There is no obviously correct way to do this. You might consider the direct increase in sales that will arise for your planned up-sell or cross-sell features as an indicator. Alternatively, you may feel that the benefit to be gained from collaboration with customers is so important that the monetary benefit is equivalent to the cost of losing that customer altogether. Only you can estimate the real benefits of this type of feature for your unique company and business situation. Bear in mind, though, that you must be able to justify the level of benefit you perceive to other stakeholders in the business.

Again, to provide a useful, concise summary of the cost–benefit analysis, you should prepare a *pro forma* cash flow projection for your solution. An example is shown in Table 3-3.

Table 3-3.   An Example Cash Flow Projection

	Year 1	Year 2	Year 3
Implementation costs	(75,000)		
Operating costs	(80,000)	(82,000)	(84,000)
Benefits	800,000	820,000	840,000
Net cash flow	645,000	738,000	756,000

Bear in mind that, at this stage, you have only *estimated* costs and benefits. There are always some risks involved for each part of your estimate. These risks should be identified and then accounted for in one way or another.

Identifying Risks

You can categorize the risks that affect your use of technology in part of a business strategy into the following types:

- **Alignment risk.** The IT solution you propose might not align as well as you think it will with the other business strategies of your company.

- **Implementation risk.** Costs associated with implementing a given solution can often vary from initial estimates, such as the number of staff hours needed to roll out the products, or payment to consultants and developers.

- **Operating risk.** As with implementation risks, the costs associated with operating a certain solution might vary from the original projection. For example, there might be a more involved administrative requirement than initially anticipated.

- **Solution risk.** There is a possibility that any given solution may carry unforeseen risks, such as reliability issues, downtime required for maintenance, and so on.

- **Benefit risk.** We have described how some of the benefits of your solution are difficult to quantify. These difficulties can lead to benefit risks, where your company does not achieve the improvements to the level you originally predicted. Additionally, forces outside of your control, such as market trends, can affect even your most careful estimates. These risks need to be taken into account.

After you have prepared your cash-flow projections, you need to analyze the types of risk that can affect your estimates. A useful approach to documenting risks may be to compile a risk assessment table. For example, you might define risk factors on a scale of 1 (low) to 5 (high) that can then be assigned to each category of risk. You should support the risk factor for each category with a statement that describes the risk. Table 3-4 is an example of a risk assessment table.

Table 3-4. An Example Risk Assessment

Risk Category	Risk Factor	Supporting Statement
Alignment risk	1.0	Stakeholders agree that the solution addresses the CSFs
Implementation risk	2.0	Some implementation issues are still unknown
Operating risk	2.0	May need more administrative staff for this solution
Solution risk	1.5	Solution may require periodic maintenance
Benefit risk	2.5	Some benefit estimates may not be accurate

Once you have compiled your risk assessment table, you will need to decide how to report the risks as part of your business case. One approach is to adjust the cash-flow projection to take the risks into account. Another is to produce best-case, worst-case, and medium-case scenarios as part of the cash-flow projections. Alternatively, you may decide to simply present a separate risk assessment table as part of your final business case, leaving the cash-flow projections unaffected by risk.

Assembling the Business Case

After you have been through all the steps described so far, you will need to assemble your business case so that you can present it to the other key stakeholders. The way in which you do this is largely a matter of personal (or corporate) preference, but our advice is to use metrics that are understood by your colleagues. Where possible, you should present measures similar to those used in your company to assess marketing campaigns, sales initiatives, research and development, and so on.

If there is no corporate standard for presenting such material, you could initially design your document using the key steps we have described as major headings, and then evolve that design to meet your needs more fully. Similarly, you could use our key steps as slide titles in a presentation.

Summary: How Suppliers Can Use Technology as a Strategic Weapon

In this chapter, we have argued that as B2B e-commerce becomes more pervasive, you share similar concerns and goals with all other suppliers, regardless of your size or complexity. Although your exact requirements may well be unique, you need to incorporate technology with your other business strategies to thrive and compete effectively in today's business environment. If you accept this basic precept, you have the right base on which to make effective decisions. Making sound decisions demands that you have a realistic view of where your company is now, and also that you have a clear idea of where you need to take it in the not-too-distant future. You need to take into account your interactions with customers and trading partners, but you should not ignore how this will affect your employees. Ideally, you want to empower your workforce so that they carry any solution forward to maximum benefit for all concerned.

You will need to assess the costs of including technology as part of your business strategy against the benefits that you predict it will reap. Not only should you do this for your own peace of mind, but you may also have to convince other key stakeholders at your company of the wisdom of using technology to revolutionize the way your organization carries out its business. We have provided a brief overview of a framework that can help you do just that.

The success of your initiative to use technology as a strategic weapon for your business depends on the suitability of the solution you commission. We will provide you with some guidance about what to look for in *Chapter 4, "Business Strategies and Solutions,"* but it is up to you to match functionality, such as sell-side features, remote shopping, front-end integration, and back-end integration, with your particular needs.

We are convinced that the appropriate use of technology can do more than improve efficiency, reduce costs, and increase revenue. Intelligently applied, it can be used to revolutionize the way in which you do business with your trading partners and customers. You can place yourself firmly at the center of your relationships and you can have your customers as dependent on your particular organization as you are on theirs. They will find the collaboration and value-added information that you can provide as indispensable as you find the money that they spend with you.

Business Strategies and Solutions

By this stage, you should be convinced of the need to gain a competitive advantage (or at least to avoid disadvantage) by automating links between your organization and your business customers. We have discussed the major benefits that you can achieve through such automation and the sort of value that you can add to the interactions with your trading partners. Our key objective now is to turn all of these fine words and ideas into something tangible.

Throughout this chapter and the next, we use case studies to examine how particular companies have approached and implemented successful business-to-business (B2B) e-commerce strategies. This should help give you further insight into how you can apply the strategies and solutions described in these chapters. We will start by examining the building blocks on which you can base your particular strategy, and we will help you to identify what you need to achieve from this strategy. We will then discuss the range of available solutions and help you to identify both the benefits and disadvantages of the particular types. The most important topic we will examine is how you can identify the most appropriate solution for your unique business needs and considerations.

Note that there is a certain "chicken and egg" situation when discussing strategy and solutions. Without a grasp of what can be achieved with existing solutions, it is difficult to set a realistic strategy. Equally, without an understanding of the strategy to be pursued, it is difficult to appreciate the pros and cons of different solutions. Because of this, this chapter takes several sweeps through the strategy and solutions landscape, first giving you background on what is possible and some of the benefits, costs, and trade-offs involved. We then delve deeper into particular strategies and solutions as we examine how they are applied in common cases.

Case Studies

It is commonly said that a picture is worth a thousand words. In trying to explain how e-commerce strategies and solutions can improve your business, we hope the following set of case studies has a similar effect. These case studies examine the way in which real companies approached the assessment of strategies and solutions, as well as provide an insight into the motivation behind their choices. The following sections provide an introduction to the different companies used as the basis for the case studies in this chapter and the next. As you look through them, you may well find that the challenges they faced seem familiar.

TCS Corporate Services

TCS Corporate Services supplies large organizations with computer printer sales and servicing, remanufactured printer toner cartridges, scanners, faxes, and general office supplies. Although it occupies only about 1 percent of its chosen industry, TCS is one of the largest players in its market.

Several of TCS's major customers indicated that they would expect their suppliers to start conducting transactions through new e-procurement systems or risk losing the business. This left TCS with the task of bringing its business, and its 25,000 associated products, online in a very short time.

In addition to satisfying immediate and specific customer requirements, TCS wanted to enter the e-commerce arena for many reasons. This would allow them to gain new customers and to retain existing customers who wished to implement electronic purchasing applications in the future.

MarkMaster

MarkMaster is a family-owned, $5 million company that manufactures rubber stamps for various customers, including large financial institutions and insurance companies. Its products are highly customized, requiring the correct spelling, fonts, colors, and so on. A single error renders the product useless, but the products have a low unit cost of about $5.

Case Studies   *(continued)*

The company realized that it had to address several issues with its existing customer interactions:

- The customer would fill out an order form and then fax or mail it to MarkMaster. Each paper order was processed by one of eight full-time order entry clerks.

- 6000 of these paper orders were handled per day, and a large spike occurred every day to handle overnight fulfillment promises.

- Some orders were found to be incomplete or unreadable. The error rate was about 1 percent, which equates to 60 orders per day!

- Large customers were beginning to move away from paper orders toward automated procurement systems and other purchasing applications.

The overall situation is summarized in Figure 4-1.

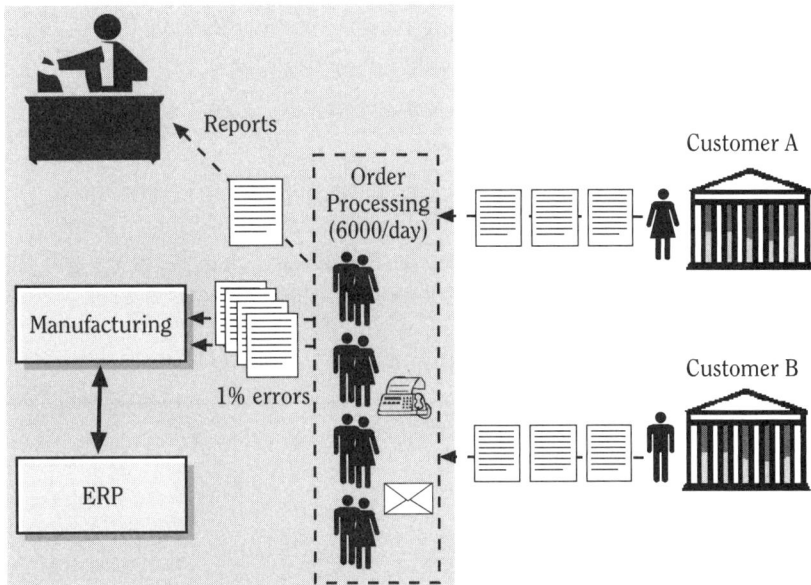

Figure 4-1.   *"Before" at MarkMaster.*

(continued)

Case Studies   (continued)

MarkMaster needed to maintain the high level of customization associated with its products, but at the same time it needed to reduce the error rate and provide integrated solutions for those customers that were moving to automated procurement systems.

Lamons Gasket

Lamons Gasket is an $80 million company. It is the largest supplier of static sealing solutions to the petrochemical, refining, paper, and other industries. It manufactures and distributes more than 100,000 standard and special order products.

The ordering process at Lamons Gasket, before automation, makes interesting reading:

- Orders were received primarily by phone or fax and were dealt with by one of 30 customer service representatives. They translated these orders into Lamons' internal format, and this data was then entered manually into its enterprise resource planning (ERP) system by a team of order entry clerks.

- The order entry clerks were handling 500 orders per day, each of which took an average of 30 minutes to process.

- The approximate error rate was 1 percent, so on average, 5 orders per day were incorrect.

- If customers insisted on using electronic data interchange (EDI), the EDI documents were printed and routed through the manual process already described. An integrated EDI solution was considered too expensive for Lamons Gasket.

The overall situation is summarized in Figure 4-2.

Case Studies   *(continued)*

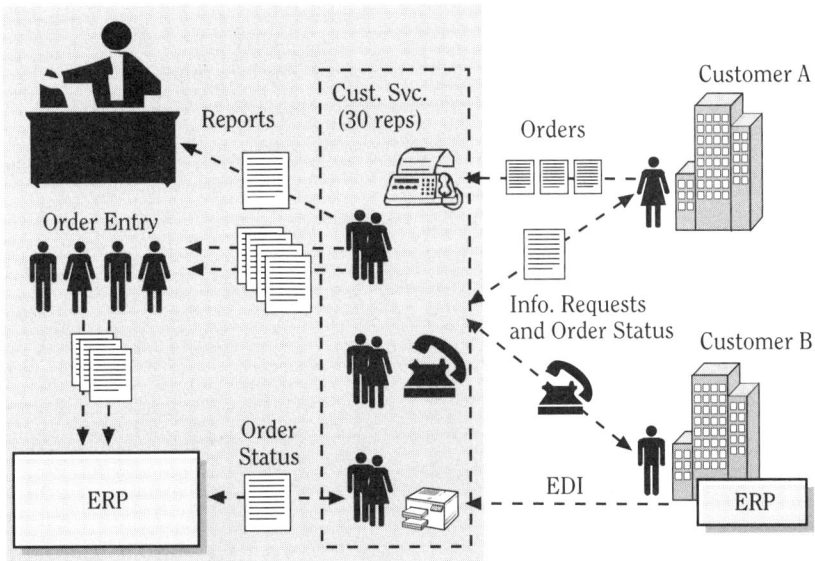

Figure 4-2. *"Before" at Lamons Gasket.*

The primary impetus for Lamons Gasket was thus twofold: to reduce the costs and potential for error associated with the manual processing of sales orders, and also to provide a flexible solution that could handle customer demand for technology-based solutions, such as EDI.

Equilon Lubricants

Equilon Lubricants, a $1.4 billion joint venture between Shell Oil Company and Texaco, Inc., is a business unit of Equilon Enterprises. Equilon Lubricants sells oil-based products such as motor oil, coolants, and antifreeze directly to major corporations such as Schlumberger and General Motors, as well as its large chain of retailers.

Although Equilon had previously invested in an electronic B2B solution, the management realized that improvement was still needed:

- An existing EDI system was being used to integrate with large customers.

(continued)

Case Studies *(continued)*

- The product ordering process was not simple to automate. For example, some of Equilon's products are very heavy, so the price of a product could vary substantially depending on the location of the customer and the delivery channel used.

- Despite the existence of the EDI system, there was still a lot of paper being passed as part of the ordering process, leading to inefficiency and potential for errors.

The overall situation is summarized in Figure 4-3.

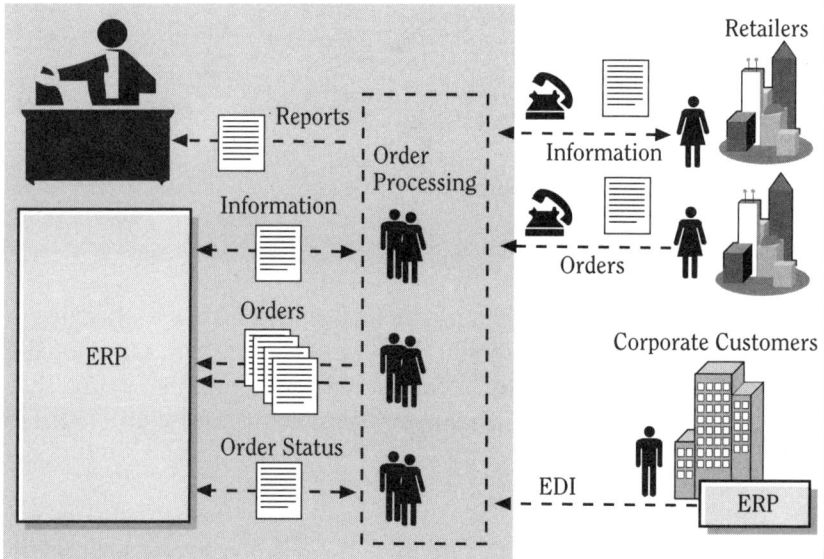

Figure 4-3.   *"Before" at Equilon Lubricants.*

Equilon Lubricants wanted to improve customer satisfaction by integrating its systems with those of its customers. This would reduce the amount of manual order processing required and hence reduce costs.

Selecting a Strategy

The strategies that you can adopt for the automation of B2B processes range in scope from simply allowing customers to access your catalog data up to allowing highly sophisticated interactions with automated procurement systems or marketplaces. However, this is not a simple sliding scale against which your organization's requirements can be measured. Rather, you need to form an individual strategy by a making a series of decisions about the desired results, the level of functionality you require, and the various types of cost associated with implementing that functionality.

As an example, consider an organization that wants to be integrated with a particular business customer that it perceives as key to its success. The senior management team may be willing to invest in a solution that delivers tight integration with that particular customer's e-procurement system by buying appropriate products and infrastructure. However, they would not necessarily be willing to invest further to expand this functionality to all of their customers or to expand to additional sales channels such as B2B marketplaces. For these other customers and markets, the organization may provide a simple online shopping site. This would reduce the overall cost of its B2B e-commerce initiative while still delivering the critical functionality to its overall customer base. In short, the organization will apply different strategies to different segments of its market.

You, too, will probably require different strategies to integrate with your various customers. Therefore, you must first determine what type of functionality you want to deliver.

Building Blocks

In *Chapter 2, "Business-to-Business E-Commerce Objectives for Suppliers,"* we described many of the functional requirements that suppliers perceive as necessary to deliver a powerful and flexible solution. This functionality can be broadly categorized as follows:

- Catalog. The storage and management of product information in an electronic catalog is central to most supplier solutions. Some of this information will be reasonably static (such as part number and product description) and other parts will be dynamic (such as price or availability). Also important is your ability to present custom catalogs and pricing to different customers. For example, a certain customer may attract a specific discount level, so all pricing information must be adjusted appropriately for that specific customer.

- **Publishing.** Catalogs must also be made available to customers and customer purchasing applications, usually across the Internet. The catalog information must be published in a format that suits the customer, such as Hypertext Markup Language (HTML) pages on your Web site or a dialect of Extensible Markup Language (XML) for use by an application. If a customer application receives a copy of the catalog information, there must be some way to validate the information and control the frequency with which it is updated.

- **Sell-side integration.** Certain types of functionality will help you integrate more easily with customer systems and still allow your customers to differentiate between your products and those of your competitors. One example of this is the ability to provide remote shopping features for your customers. In this case, the information presented may need to vary dynamically based on the identity of the person accessing it. For example, you might want to limit the types of products or services made available during the remote shopping session or alter the options for configurable products.

- **Integration with existing technology investments.** Integrating with your customers' systems is of limited use if the mechanism used does not integrate with your own business systems. Many solutions will require integration with at least your accounting, product, inventory, and fulfillment systems, and potentially also with your sales and customer relationship management (CRM) systems.

- **Order management.** For orders to be submitted electronically, there must be a mechanism in place to receive and process them, either locally or through existing order management systems. You may also want to provide customers with the ability to track the status of their orders.

- **Multiple channels.** Unless the potential market is very limited, you will want to interact with customers' procurement applications and custom applications and through electronic marketplaces, using industry standard protocols or possibly custom mechanisms, all from the same application.

- **Business intelligence.** Because most organizations continually strive to better understand the needs and behaviors of their customers and control their own inventory costs, you may require features that allow your company to collect, analyze, and present information about buying patterns and the like.

- **Transformation.** Although most new e-commerce protocols are based on XML, there are still many different dialects that can be adopted by different business partners in different industries. Core to any solution is its ability to transform between the XML dialect(s) used within your organization and those used by your trading partners, including non-XML formats such as EDI.

- **Business process integration.** As the relationship between customer and supplier moves beyond simple order submission, you may wish to extend the business process flow between your company and your trading partners. This could involve the choreography of the exchanges involved in ordering (purchase orders, invoices, and various receipts) or the management of sophisticated interactions during remote shopping.

- **Messaging.** Probably the most successful application on the Internet is e-mail. E-mail has the immediacy of a telephone call (well, almost) but is still delivered even if the recipient is not there. Once it is safely stored in the recipient's inbound message queue, an e-mail message can be handled at a later time when it is convenient. The same principle applies to many B2B messages, as not all B2B e-commerce systems are available 24 hours a day, 7 days a week. Some systems may operate at reduced capacity during off-peak periods or at maintenance time. Hence, some solutions will provide routing and queuing of business messages in the same way that your company e-mail system provides this functionality for your e-mail messages.

The need for any particular functionality and the level of sophistication will vary depending on the objectives of the strategy and the context in which that strategy will be implemented.

Building Blocks at MarkMaster

The solution implemented to support the desired strategy at Mark-Master required several of the functional building blocks in our list:

- A catalog that would contain information on the company's 400+ products.

- Publication of detailed product information so that customers can place their own orders electronically.

- Customers would access MarkMaster products through e-marketplaces or company-specific automated procurement systems, so sell-side integration in the MarkMaster solution was to include remote shopping functionality that would bring customers to the MarkMaster Web site. Once a customer had finished examining product details and had configured an order, the completed order would then be delivered back to the procurement application or marketplace. This would enable MarkMaster to retain control of how its products are represented and ensure that customers are aware of the specific value uniquely associated with Mark-Master's products.

- Integration with existing ERP and business systems, including its own homegrown MasterTrac manufacturing system.

- Order management functionality to handle the receipt of purchase orders from customer or partner purchasing applications. These orders would be converted and automatically transferred into the company's order management and manufacturing systems.

- The MarkMaster solution would service many customers through multiple channels with a single implementation. This would enable the company to sell its products directly to multiple customer procurement applications and through several different e-marketplaces.

Building Blocks at MarkMaster *(continued)*

- Once the customer has created an order on MarkMaster's site, it would be submitted to the originating purchasing application for approval. This would involve transformation into the appropriate format required by the originating site. Similarly, incoming orders would also be transformed into an appropriate format for further processing.

- Business process integration with customer applications would be delivered as part of the remote shopping functionality. The MarkMaster site would effectively become part of the customer's application, in terms of both user perception and business process flow.

As you can see, even a small enterprise such as MarkMaster required a fairly sophisticated solution because its overall intention was to execute on multiple strategies to meet the needs of different customers. Hence, the overall functionality of the solution is determined by the requirements of the largest customers to which they supply. As Kevin Govin, chief operating officer (COO) of MarkMaster, relates, "Our largest customers told us that we need to be able to accommodate their e-procurement initiatives if we want to keep their business." An examination of the different customers' requirements led to the implemented solution that "enables MarkMaster to service its customers in the manner that they prefer—through the e-procurement sites they're all moving towards."

Setting Objectives

In an ideal world, every organization wishing to engage in B2B trading would provide all of the rich functionality listed in the previous section. However, this is not the case in the real world for two main reasons:

- In many cases, such a range of functionality would far exceed that which is useful to most customers. Although some sophisticated customers might be able to exploit much of the functionality provided, others might only be able to take advantage of a small fraction.

- Each additional piece of functionality that you provide has associated costs. These go beyond the simple monetary costs of implementation to include factors such as time to market, resource availability (can you find the right people with the right skills to develop or manage the solution?), and ongoing maintenance costs.

Therefore, each organization must assess its ideal objectives in terms of its capabilities and the context in which it operates. Just like any form of business planning, a strategy for B2B automation must be considered in terms of the benefits it delivers and the costs it incurs.

Setting Objectives at Equilon Lubricants

When deciding on objectives at Equilon Lubricants, the company looked to improve the efficiency of existing processes and add new services above and beyond its existing customer interactions. Its objectives included the following:

- Delivering enriched customer services using the Internet as a delivery mechanism.

- Allowing customers to use automated procurement systems and submit electronic orders. These orders would then be handled directly by Equilon's internal ERP system.

- Providing a range of catalogs and product information to suit the needs of Equilon's corporate customers.

- Providing dynamic pricing to allow for variations in customer location, distribution channel, and so forth.

- Reducing the transaction costs associated with the manual processes by 10 to 15 percent.

- Providing access through e-marketplaces as required by some customers.

Such a vision requires a high level of functionality. However, by choosing the appropriate partners and products, Equilon Lubricants implemented a solution meeting these objectives in just six weeks.

Keeping Things in Context

All organizations are different. They differ in the products they offer, the way they do business, the revenue they generate, the infrastructure they own, the number of people they employ, and the skills of those people. This provides the context in which any strategy must be executed. Similarly, the objectives that organizations associate with their B2B e-commerce strategy will differ. Some will wish to make it easier for existing customers to do business with them, whereas others may perceive it as a way to enter new markets quickly and with minimum investment.

Objectives and context will differ from organization to organization. There is no single automated B2B solution that satisfies all organizations. However, you can work out your objectives and then decide on a strategy that fits your particular context.

Consider a fictitious company that sells office supplies. Imagine that it already has an existing network of sales representatives in its various sales districts. If a business objective is to increase sales by 50 percent, it could take one of several paths:

1. Increase the number of salespeople in each district by 50 percent. This would achieve the objective while carrying on the organization's existing sales strategy. Costs will generally increase in line with the number of sales representatives recruited. However, if one or more sales districts were at or near saturation, increasing the number of sales representatives would have little effect.

2. Expand into new sales districts not currently served by the network of sales representatives. If the company is lucky, these districts are crying out for more sources of office supplies. However, it is more likely that this move would involve additional costs, as time must be spent making inroads into this new territory. This may involve significant marketing and advertising efforts and may have to be pursued in the face of existing competition.

3. Provide an online ordering service for office supplies. This would scale far better than the existing sales mechanism, because no new sales representatives would be needed and the solution would have global reach. However, marketing would still be required to inform potential customers of this new source of office supplies. Also, are there mechanisms in place to deal with shipping appropriate

quantities to different locations, possibly in different countries with export rules and different tax scenarios? Does the organization have sufficient IT staff to develop and maintain such a site? How does the organization deal with existing customers who want to interact directly over the Web rather than through the traditional sales chan-nel(s)? Who will explain this to that particular sales representative?

In all three of these cases, the objective was the same, but the strategy was different. In each case (after the word *however*) there was a list of issues that needed to be tackled to implement that strategy. Strategy 1 will be the most familiar to those involved, and thus probably the simplest one to execute. This would require more money invested in the sales process to hire new sales rep-resentatives and would require some business intelligence to determine how saturated the existing sales districts are. If these two conditions were met, it would be reasonably straightforward to implement.

Conversely, Strategy 3 is the most complex. Before pursuing this strategy, far more questions must be answered. These include technical questions about how to deliver the Web-based solution, operational questions about the fit of this solution with existing business practices and capacity, and human questions of how it all fits with the existing business practices.

The existing sales force, the saturation level of existing territories, and the ability to ship products to distant locations all form part of the context in which the strategy must be determined. To pursue a particular strategy, our fictional organization must either select a strategy to suit the context or change the context to match the strategy. In some cases, such as the satura-tion level of existing sales territories, there is little the organization can do to change the context. In other cases, such as a lack of trained IT staff, the orga-nization could change the context by recruiting or retraining IT staff, or it could adjust part of the implementation by using external resources to create or host the desired solution. Remember, however, that whether internal or external, IT resources still cost money.

Some of the context in which a business operates is very much company-specific and therefore largely outside the scope of this book. However, when we examine the area of B2B e-commerce, it is clear that there are forces that are common to many organizations. Examples of the forces that can be identi-fied and addressed include the following:

- The budget available to implement and maintain any strategy and its associated solution(s).

- The number and level of IT staff with the required skills.

- Whether existing or potential customers are capable of taking advantage of any new strategy or solution.

- The need to integrate with solutions currently used by potential or existing customers.

- The existence of competition in the market.

- The existence of marketplaces for trading the particular products and services.

- How well a particular strategy ties in with your existing sales processes.

- If you currently differentiate your products and services in a particular way (your unique selling point), whether a particular strategy fits with these differentiators.

The last point is important to bear in mind. If your business is built on a high level of customer care and flexibility, a lot of thought must go into a potential online replacement or addition to your sales and service.

Context at Lamons Gasket

Consider some of the context under which Lamons Gasket needed to implement a B2B e-commerce strategy:

- Orders must be fed into an existing ERP system to be fulfilled.

- A high level of order accuracy is required, because many products are built to order, ranging in price from $1 to $8000.

- The company operates 13 regional sales and distribution centers across the United States and Canada.

- Its customers are large industrial companies such as Exxon, Dow, Shell, and BP Amoco, as well as independent distributors to these same companies.

- The level of sophistication of customer order submission ranges from telephone orders to full EDI exchange.

- The company has an in-house IT staff of four people.

(continued)

> **Context at Lamons Gasket**   *(continued)*
>
> The impact on strategy of certain factors can be seen almost immediately. For example, because of the type of product being ordered, a rich interaction with the customer is required to successfully replace the human interaction in the process.
>
> Conversely, some aspects of the solution or its implementation can be derived from this context. For example, it is highly unlikely that the company will try to implement its own solution with an IT staff of four unless it seeks outside assistance.

Striking a Balance

As you can see, the key to a successful strategy is to balance aspirations with operational realities. You cannot make decisions about which strategy to pursue in a vacuum. It is important, therefore, to categorize objectives into those that are essential and those that are "nice to have." It is important to quantify any objectives where possible, because the difference between processing, say, 500 commodity sales per day and processing thousands of custom build-to-order sales per day may demand that you migrate from a simple, packaged solution to a sophisticated and highly scalable one.

The Sliding Scale of Solutions

As mentioned earlier, there is no "one size fits all" strategy for B2B e-commerce. The same applies to technology-based solutions. These solutions can range from simple, packaged solutions hosted by third parties to complex, custom-tailored solutions supported by dedicated infrastructure. Each organization, from a small business through to a multinational corporation, must identify its requirements and context to select a solution that delivers the appropriate functionality and benefits.

Once the type and level of functionality has been determined, appropriate solutions can be identified and their costs assessed compared to the benefits that they would bring. This in itself may lead to a reassessment of the required functionality if the cost exceeds expectations or the intended benefits will not be delivered.

One thing to remember as you consider the following options is that you do not have to do everything at once. Small organizations, in particular, may want or need to start small and add features and capacity as their business grows. It is this type of scalability and extensibility that is key to any long-term solution, so the important thing is to choose a solution that is capable of a phased approach and short-term gains, even if you are only currently exploiting a few of the possibilities.

Solution Complexity

Figure 4-4 reflects the sliding scale of solutions that can be applied in pursuit of your desired strategy. It represents the general range of solutions to support increasingly sophisticated strategies, from simple browser-based services through hosted solutions and on to fully integrated e-business solutions. Although it is a useful representation, the figure should not be taken as an absolute statement, but as a general guide.

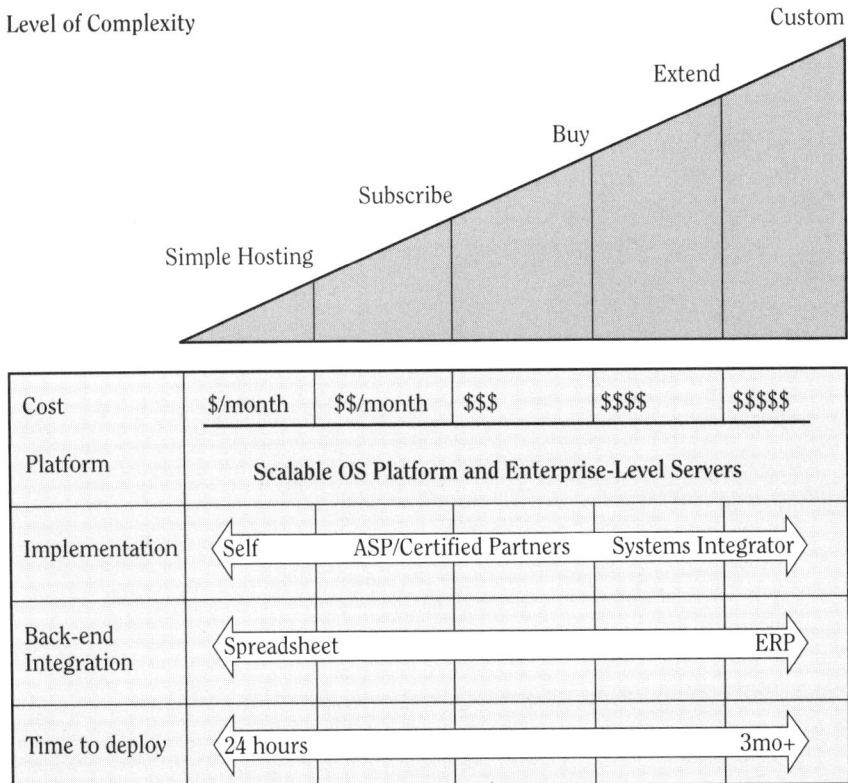

Cost	$/month	$$/month	$$$	$$$$	$$$$$
Platform	Scalable OS Platform and Enterprise-Level Servers				
Implementation	⟨Self	ASP/Certified Partners		Systems Integrator⟩	
Back-end Integration	⟨Spreadsheet				ERP⟩
Time to deploy	⟨24 hours				3mo+⟩

Figure 4-4.   *A sliding scale of solution complexity.*

Solutions can be identified and categorized by their principal attributes or the style of implementation. As the type of solution changes, so does the level of complexity.

Solution types are discussed in more detail over the next few sections, but as a general rule, the simplest solutions require the least development effort and lowest budget, and they can be delivered very rapidly. Such solutions are the least tailored to the organization and its customers, providing only minimal integration with the organization's own systems and less in the way of competitive differentiation.

As the solutions grow more sophisticated, dedicated resources are generally applied to deliver increased levels of integration with back-office applications and differentiated customer service. These resources take the form of enterprise-level server software that provides both e-commerce and integration capabilities. The cost of the increased sophistication comes in terms of increased time frames for delivery, higher levels of development skill required, and significantly more money invested in development and maintenance.

It is worth noting the following at this point:

- To be scalable, all solutions should be underpinned by enterprise-class operating systems and servers—we term this the *e-commerce platform*. The e-commerce platform should also provide sufficient extensibility to support changes in strategy as they occur. If a solution is implemented on an unsuitable platform, the only way to achieve the newly required functionality may be to throw away the existing application and platform and start again from scratch.

- The implementation strategy of having your solution hosted by a third party is not limited to any particular size or complexity of solution. As we will discuss later, it is just as possible to outsource the hosting and maintenance of a complex solution as a simple one. The issue of third-party hosting is really orthogonal to the level of complexity.

- As the level of complexity increases, so does the cost. Simple solutions tend to cost significantly less than more sophisticated ones, especially if they are hosted by third parties. The likelihood that some or all of a simple solution will be outsourced is reflected in the use of cost per month in Figure 4-4.

The remainder of this section explores the solution types on this sliding scale.

Simple Hosted Solutions

When any small business starts up, it will typically not be able to do every-thing itself. There are many things to be done, such as finding office space; setting it up with power, telephones, and heating; and employing someone to answer the phone. All of this can be a large overhead for a very small company, as it may not initially be able to afford a long lease or to employ a receptionist. If the company does commit itself to a long-term lease, a phase of rapid growth may see it expand beyond the confines of its original office, requiring more effort to house new workers and possibly a move to a new location.

In response to these types of issues, a market has sprung up in the provision of serviced office space, sometimes referred to as *executive suites*. A company can rent a serviced office, complete with power, heat, light, telephones, and sometimes Internet connectivity, all for a simple monthly fee. The company has minimal dealings with the service suppliers and can share resources, such as receptionists, photocopiers, and so forth, with other occupants of the building. When the company grows, it can frequently rent more space in the same build-ing from the organization that provides the serviced office space. The company can therefore pay for just the right level of accommodation it needs until it feels able to take on its own office space.

The same principles apply to first steps into e-commerce. Regardless of the size of your company, you may not initially know what types of service you want to provide or how many of your customers will want to make use of such services. In this case, you would want the e-commerce equivalent of the serviced office, in which someone takes care of the infrastructure and provides you with a simple set of service options from which you can choose. E-commerce hosting companies provide this type of solution, allowing you to choose from a simple selection of e-commerce services to suit your initial requirements. As with the serviced office, the e-commerce hosting company must be able to scale with your organization until you feel comfortable striking out on your own. Indeed, if your e-commerce needs are reasonably uncomplicated, a simple hosted e-commerce solution may be all you require.

Note   In this section we are intentionally using the term *simple hosted e-commerce solution*. Almost all of the solutions discussed in this book can be partially or completely outsourced to a third party to install, configure, and maintain. As such, the concept of hosting applies all across the scale. The spe-cific area we are examining here is where an e-commerce hosting company provides a fixed set of standard options from which you can choose to create your e-commerce presence.

How Does Simple Hosting Work?

Under the simple hosting model, the e-commerce hosting company offers a fixed set of standard options from which you can choose. A small amount of customization will take place to make the solution more specific to your company, such as the use of your company name and logo, a company-specific Web address through which it can be accessed, and cosmetic changes such as selecting how the applications look (often from a fixed set of styles). You will be able to select as much or as little of the functionality offered as you like. This usually starts with a basic hosting package offering a Web presence and e-mail capability. You can then add capabilities such as Web-based shopping and payment, although the hosting company will house all of the information and processes required for this. There will be little, if any, chance for integration with your existing computer systems or your business processes.

Pros and Cons of Simple Hosted Solutions

The main advantage of a simple hosted solution is that it requires minimal up-front investment from you to establish an e-commerce presence. You will typically pay for the services on a monthly basis and you can potentially switch hosting companies should you require new or extended functionality that your current hosting company does not offer. You will need to put some time and effort into setting up the service, but the hosting company generally makes this very simple for you. All concerns about product and solution selection, maintenance, scalability, availability, and so on sit squarely with the hosting company.

The price you pay for simplicity comes in two forms:

- The solution is limited in functionality. On one side, there is a limit to the functionality provided to help you sell to and integrate with your customers. On the other side, there is a limit to the amount of integration with your own systems and processes.

- Because you can only select from a standard set of services, there is obviously a lack of differentiation from other companies using the same hosting service (and most other hosting services). You only have a small amount of control over what is provided and how it is delivered.

If you require a more sophisticated or integrated solution, you should consider a more sophisticated, yet still subscription-based, application you have identified as being key to your strategy.

Subscription-Based Applications

Returning to the small business example, it may be that a company is reasonably self-sufficient in most ways but will turn to specialists in specific areas. An example of this would be accountancy services, in which the small business is provided with ongoing taxation and salary information over the course of the year. The company works with the accountancy firm to set up accounting systems that are streamlined to the company's specific requirements. The relationship between the accountancy firm and the company will usually be deeper than that of the company and a serviced office provider.

In e-commerce terms, more sophisticated hosting companies can host dedicated applications for you that can be configured far more closely to your requirements than those of a simple hosted solution.

How Do Subscription-Based Applications Work?

In the most common scenario, it is possible to rent e-commerce facilities from an application service provider (ASP) who will host and manage the e-commerce software. You will be able to integrate these rented facilities with your existing systems to a greater or lesser degree to create the overall e-commerce application. In some cases, the rented services may form the whole of your application.

The applications that can be rented include packaged software such as e-commerce platforms, ERP systems, accountancy packages, and collaboration software. Other facilities can be rented, from raw disk space on a server, through space in a database, to the ability to run server-side Web functionality.

As part of the subscription agreement for such facilities, you will usually have options to configure features so that they do the following:

- Deliver the required functionality for your application.

- Integrate with your existing systems in a far more sophisticated way than is possible with a simple hosted solution.

- Conform to your corporate style and business processes.

The ASP may target this type of service at all sizes of enterprises that do not have the expertise, budget, or desire to host such applications themselves. The ASP will be able to spread the cost of the hosting infrastructure and application support specialists across those organizations that subscribe to the applications.

In some cases, further cost reductions can be made by sharing a single copy of an application between multiple companies. This provides more configurability than a simple hosted solution, but the shared nature will potentially impose flexibility and scalability limitations compared to having a dedicated solution.

Pros and Cons of Subscribing to Applications

The benefits of subscribing to applications mainly involve cost and IT resources. Renting the application removes the up-front cost of buying and installing the application. Renting also removes the need to have the IT expertise to install, configure, and maintain the applications.

The downsides of renting an application relate to ongoing cost and lack of flexibility. Although you have minimized the up-front cost associated with the application, you have the expense of an ongoing subscription fee, which may exceed, over time, the cost of buying, installing, and maintaining the application yourself. The fact that the application is hosted at a remote site may well limit the amount of integration that is possible with your existing systems. Also, the often-shared nature of the service imposes limitations on the levels of configuration and integration available. There are also risks regarding security and capacity that must be assessed when sharing an application with another company.

Implementing Packaged Applications

As your need for flexibility grows, it may make more sense for your organization to install and configure particular applications to have control over their precise implementation and execution. This can deliver far higher levels of integration with your own business practices and existing systems.

Using Packaged Applications

Packaged applications will provide a cross-section of the functionality that you may require to pursue your B2B e-commerce strategies. If you are prepared to install, configure, and maintain your own applications, you will retain complete control over which applications you choose and how you configure them. You can often choose solutions that provide more functionality than those available for rent. This could allow you to deliver a richer interaction with customers and with their applications, such as more sophisticated remote shopping. Alternatively, you may wish to improve your operations and sell into new markets by taking advantage of product-specific adapters for different customer applications. Plug-in components may be available to provide additional functionality, such as analytical tools that can help you assess and guide your online business.

Although you will be taking responsibility for selection and installation of the software, the server machines on which the software resides may be hosted either with a service provider or at your organization's own site. Using a service provider has potential benefits in that you can take advantage of its expertise in delivering highly available and scalable hardware configurations. You can also benefit from its infrastructure in terms of the size and reliability of the connection it has to the Internet, which may far exceed that of your own organization. The decision to use a service provider (or not) can be made independently of the overall decision to install and configure your own applications.

Pros and Cons of Packaged Applications

The benefits of implementing your own applications are largely in terms of flexibility and control. You can configure the application as you want and you retain complete control over the security and capacity of the application. Going further, you can install and configure applications that may not be available by subscription.

Another aspect to consider is that the application hosting market is a reasonably recent phenomenon. Such applications are not yet proven in all situations; hence, you may feel more secure implementing your own version rather than renting.

The downside to this approach is that you must provide sufficient IT skills (internal or outsourced) to install and maintain the solution, even if it is hosted by a service provider, if you are to see any significant advantage over a rented solution. You must also pay up front for the software and fund any ongoing license fees together with the IT staff costs. You will also be responsible for ensuring that the application is available when your customers want it (what happens if there is a hardware failure?) and that it scales to meet demand. Building systems that are highly scalable and available is not a simple task, which is why you may wish to refer to an external expert, whether that is a consultant or a service provider.

Extending the Solution

There is a broad range of packaged software applications available, and this range is growing by the day. However, there is no guarantee that there will be an application that can meet all the needs of your organization.

Customizing Applications

When you examine the available products and solutions to see which match your requirements, you may discover that the only one that matches all requirements is too expensive and may provide features that you do not need. A less expensive application may meet most of the needs, but would require custom business logic or components to deliver the desired solution. Given the context of your organization and the level of IT skills you have available, you may decide to develop your own solution based on the lower cost applications rather than losing the functionality altogether.

This type of decision may be taken out of your hands if business requirements change. For example, if a new procurement or marketplace application is deployed by your customer(s), the vendor of your e-commerce solution may not provide integration facilities with that customer application in the time frame you require. As such, extensibility and the associated tools are critical for success.

The solution often begins with packaged applications that are then added to or customized. In most cases, you will need to apply some software development or integration resources to deliver the solution you require. Alternatively, you may need to create sizable amounts of custom code to attain the desired effect. It may be best to call in the services of a solution provider or systems integrator with a track record of delivering such systems rather than to go it alone. Such partners may know of common solution configurations. This knowledge may not only speed up implementation immeasurably, but it is also a guarantee that the solution has been tested and proven to work— there is no such guarantee when you are implementing a very specialized solution. All packaged products have a "sweet spot" centered on their principal functionality. As you try to extend their functionality, you may come across issues that even the product vendors themselves have not encountered, so having experience on board in this area is often critical to the success of the whole project.

Pros and Cons of Application Customization

The benefit of extending a packaged application to deliver a solution is that the solution will be far more tailored to your business needs.

The disadvantages of extending packaged applications include the need for more IT resources, both initially and on an ongoing basis. The solution will also take longer to deliver than one based on "out of the box" functionality. Adapted or extended applications can be trickier and more expensive to maintain and are often more difficult to upgrade when the next versions of the technologies on which they are based are released.

Custom Solutions

Some organizations have highly specialized or complex requirements for their solutions. This could result from pursuing a particularly sophisticated, or even an immature, market. It could also be a reflection of the company's own complex business practices and methodologies. Furthermore, the mixture of existing systems and processes may rule out the use of certain types of solutions.

As the complexity of requirements or context grows, more and more customization is needed. At the extreme, a large, global organization may build its own solutions "from the ground up" to deliver precisely the functionality it requires.

The balance between an extended solution and a custom solution lies in the depth of change required to provide the solution. As a rule, an extended solution will involve adding extra functionality around the essential "core" functions delivered by the underlying application(s). The point at which an extended solution becomes a custom solution occurs when some of the core functionality of an underlying application is replaced by custom code.

Because a custom solution is, in many ways, simply further up the scale than an extended solution, it will share many of the pros and cons of an extended solution. However, each advantage and disadvantage tends to be accentuated. For example, a custom solution can deliver extreme flexibility, but at the cost of higher maintenance. More effort will be required to update the changed parts of the application core as new versions of the underlying technologies appear. Also bear in mind that the relative cost of a custom solution will be higher, so the time required to deliver a return on investment may be longer than for a simpler solution.

Matching Strategies to Solutions

We have now looked at some of the strategies available for pursuing successful B2B e-commerce and some of the solutions available to deliver those strategies. All that remains is to match solution to strategy.

It would be easy to say that small organizations require simple solutions and large organizations require complex solutions. However, things are never that simple, as the requirements of organizations are not guaranteed to be in direct proportion to their size. Also, organizations will adjust and adapt their solutions to fit their own contexts. For example, although a large organization may require a tailored solution, that solution could be hosted and maintained by a third party to reduce the level of infrastructure and IT staff required to support the solution.

Despite the complex nature of the B2B world, it is possible to look at common solutions that are applied in response to common challenges. These solutions provide proven business models and ways of working that can be adopted for, and adapted to, your organization's requirements. The following sections describe some of the common approaches, based on the level of complexity of the requirements and the context of the organization.

Typical Low-Complexity Supplier

Suppliers who need to implement a B2B e-commerce solution with minimal overhead and cost generally adopt low-complexity solutions. Because this includes many small suppliers, you may find that such solutions are categorized elsewhere as solutions or strategies for small suppliers. However, these solutions will suit any level of supplier depending on the level of sophistication required of the solution.

Low-complexity solutions will appeal to organizations that have limited IT resources or those companies looking to "get their feet wet" and investigate the opportunity. This situation generally arises when IT does not form a major part of an organization's business. Most small companies will have a limited IT budget by nature of their size. However, some small companies whose primary focus is trading may use IT as a strategic weapon in their particular field and hence may need to implement a somewhat tailored or even custom solution. Conversely, a company specializing in the manufacture and trade of building materials may have a limited IT budget even though its trading volume would make it a "medium" enterprise rather than a small one. Such companies, for which IT may not be a key differentiator, would probably welcome the opportunity to avoid the cost involved with buying, installing, and maintaining e-commerce software and instead invest the money in its core business.

Most low-complexity solutions are delivered using the sort of hosted e-commerce solution described earlier. Such solutions have the following attributes:

- The solution is hosted by a third party. This may be an ASP or a dedicated business portal, such as Microsoft's bCentral (*http://www.bcentral.com*).

- Functionality is selected from a set of options with a small amount of tailoring required to produce an overall offering. This means that there is little or no requirement for in-house IT staff to implement and support the solution.

- The combination of the first two points means that such solutions can be delivered very quickly, often in a matter of hours.

- The cost of adopting such a solution is relatively low.

This type of solution offers a swift way of delivering a B2B e-commerce solution. The question is whether the functionality offered meets the objectives of your organization.

Features of a Hosted Solution

Typical facilities offered by hosted B2B solutions are listed here (note that this list is skewed toward those facilities most useful for B2B e-commerce rather than the outsourcing of general business applications):

- Basic Web presence, allowing customers to find and contact your organization.

- Web shopping facilities, including the presentation of product information, Web shopping cart, and credit card payment.

- Enhanced catalog facilities, including basic inventory management.

- The ability to export catalog information to procurement applications, e-marketplaces, or both.

- Limited business process integration, providing ways to streamline the online ordering mechanism with your company's payment and fulfillment mechanisms (in the case of a small business, these may also be provided by the hosting company).

- Basic business intelligence services, such as the provision of time-based or customer-based sales patterns, or information about which items are commonly bought together.

- E-mail hosting and services. This can include the maintenance of e-mail lists for customer newsletters and marketing announcements.

- Provision of business and operational applications, such as financial management software, contact management, collaboration, databases and data hosting, CRM, ERP, and so forth.

For many small organizations, it may be possible to outsource almost all applications required to run the business. If a third party already hosts key business applications, the hosting of e-commerce facilities is an even more attractive and natural choice.

Disadvantages of a Hosted Solution

A hosted solution provides a good set of entry-level services for any organization. However, the price of simplicity can be inflexibility and limitations on functionality, as described here:

- There is less room for differentiation between you and your competitors (save for those competitors who have no online presence). A good choice of hosting company can help, but there is nothing to stop your competition from also choosing similar offerings.

- Supported customer applications may vary between hosted offerings. You will only be able to select from the list provided by the hosting company, and sometimes this list can be very small.

- Complete customization is not possible. If a customer demands a link using EDI, you are at the mercy of your hosting company as to whether you can provide this facility.

- Integration with existing systems is usually quite limited. To get an online customer order into your existing ERP and sales systems may require someone to import files or read and rekey e-mail or other messages sent from the hosted e-commerce site. Similarly, it may not be possible to provide the online site with up-to-the-minute inventory levels. This may mean that customers only find out that an item is out of stock hours after they had ordered it.

- By outsourcing your e-commerce functionality, you are taking on a certain amount of risk that your hosting company will continue to evolve in step with your needs or those of your customers. It is also possible that your chosen hosting company may go out of business because of unfavorable trading conditions at some point in the future. Such risks should be assessed and managed.

Strategies Supported by a Hosted Solution

Given the type and level of functionality available from a hosted solution, you can choose from the following strategy elements:

- Online ordering and customer service through a Web-based interface. This provides a readily available and scalable interface with your customers. Customers can pay by purchase order or credit card.

- Possible integration with procurement applications and e-marketplaces. Again, the choice is limited to those provided by your hosting company or any extensibility they allow.

Obviously, if the strategies you wish to pursue go beyond these, you need to look at a more complex solution.

Hosted Solutions Using bCentral

Microsoft's bCentral business portal (*http://www.bcentral.com*) offers several options for a business wishing to provide e-commerce to its customers.

At the most basic level, a business Web site can be created to offer basic online trading capabilities. This includes product descriptions, a Web shopping cart, and simple order management. Additional useful facilities include hosted e-mail and credit card processing. This provides a good first step in terms of B2B e-commerce functionality, although it is subject to the caveats on hosted solutions laid out earlier.

bCentral provides more powerful functionality through its Commerce Manager service, which is entirely focused on online trade. Commerce Manager allows you to do the following:

- Build and maintain an online catalog either by importing product information from a suitable application, such as Microsoft Excel, or by entering details through its Web-based interface.

(continued)

Hosted Solutions Using bCentral   *(continued)*

- Publish the catalog(s) on the company's business Web site, or to different customers' automated procurement applications. Alternatively, the catalog can be published to marketplaces such as MSN Marketplace (*http://marketplace.msn.com*), eBay (*http://www.ebay.com*), eShop (*http://www.eshop.com*), and bCentral Auctions (*http://auctions.bcentral.com*).

- Provide customers with Web shopping cart functionality to keep track of orders as they browse the catalog.

- Manage orders through a central Web-based console that allows you to process orders online and track orders and inventory.

- Extract basic business intelligence such as sales history reports.

If a small business uses bCentral for its B2B e-commerce capabilities, it may also decide to take advantage of other managed business services, such as the following:

- Customer Manager, which provides a store of customer information online that can be shared by employees. It can also integrate with Commerce Manager to create a unified view of customer information.

- Microsoft SharePoint Team Services, which provides a Web site with the ability to share information and collaborate with employees and customers.

bCentral solutions are simple to use and are very inexpensive compared to other, more customized solutions. These advantages must be balanced against the limited nature of some services. However, it is possible to mix and match facilities from services such as those provided by bCentral with more powerful B2B e-commerce facilities from other sources as the business grows.

Typical Medium-Complexity Supplier

Organizations that have complex product sets, have large numbers of customers, or operate in fast-moving markets will not find sufficient functionality in a low-complexity solution to suit their needs. Typically, such organizations require a solution with one or more of the following attributes:

- The ability to sell via multiple channels, from direct Web selling, through integration with their customers' automated procurement systems, and on to participation in specific e-marketplaces.

- A higher level of customer service or differentiation than can be provided by a simple, hosted solution. This would include the provision of more sophisticated remote shopping scenarios and richer personalization.

- Increased cost savings through back-end integration with existing ERP and sales systems.

- A larger capacity for processing business transactions than is available from a simple hosted solution.

- The ability to adapt as the business requires new strategies and functionality.

As the complexity and breadth of an organization's requirements increase, so will the complexity of the solution required. This leads toward the use of a tailored solution, built on a packaged solution, and quite possibly extending that solution. Tailored solutions have the following attributes:

- The solution is based on widely available products that provide the essential building block functionality for e-commerce and integration.

- The products are combined and configured to deliver the required features and functionality. This usually involves the creation of some custom business logic to impose company-specific rules and business processes. Selecting extensible products, with powerful tools that provide for easy configuration, can minimize the amount of custom logic needed.

- The solution is implemented by experienced IT staff. This may involve in-house IT staff, consultants from a solution provider or systems integrator, or both. The solution will require some level of ongoing resources, both for maintenance and also to adapt the solution in the face of changing business requirements.

- The solution can be hosted either by the organization itself or by some form of service provider. Simpler solutions may require dedicated, hosted versions of specific software packages that are then tailored. More complex solutions may provide everything from the hardware upward. Even if the solution is implemented by in-house IT staff, you may still decide to host it with a service provider that can deliver maintenance and support 24 hours a day, 365 days a year, and can provide very high levels of availability. For example, the service provider may promise only 5 minutes of downtime a year, with compensation payable if this limit is breached. It is important to ensure that the service level agreement (SLA), which states service levels for such things as availability, has suitable provisions should the service levels be breached.

This type of solution obviously requires more resource and effort than a low-complexity solution, but the payback for more sophisticated organizations can be significant.

Features of a Tailored Solution

Typical facilities offered by tailored solutions are as follows:

- Extensive facilities for building, managing, and maintaining product catalogs.

- Catalog information can be published or exported in a variety of ways, from simple HTML for the supplier's Web site to data formats targeted at specific electronic sales channels (standard and nonstandard).

- The ability to integrate with customer applications to deliver facilities such as remote shopping. Some higher end products may provide this "out of the box," whereas simpler products will require a degree of customization to achieve this. Other common sell-side features include personalization for customers or groups of customers and the application of pricing policies to adjust prices for specific customers.

- Some back-end integration, providing two-way access to internal data sources such as databases or mainframes. Some products may provide specific adapters for popular ERP packages, such as SAP, Oracle, or Microsoft Great Plains. Other solutions may require additional custom code to achieve an appropriate level of integration.

- The ability to sell through multiple channels, based on the same underlying system. The catalog, pricing, and back-end integration functionality may all be shared by different front-ends that serve automated procurement applications, e-marketplaces, and direct customer interaction via the Web. Prebuilt adapters for different e-commerce standards may be provided to speed up integration efforts, and tools for adding new applications and channels easily are critical.

- The provision of business intelligence based on the sales flows down each sales channel. The information can be per channel or per customer, or it can be consolidated across all channels and customers.

- Enhanced transformation capabilities to convert between customer data formats and internal data formats used by the supplier. A simple hosted solution may provide this only in a limited way or only on the customer-facing side.

- All core Web presence capabilities providing a rich, personalized, and interactive experience for customers (if required).

- Web shopping facilities, including the presentation of product information, Web shopping cart, and credit card payment (if required).

Employing a tailored solution allows an organization to add value to customer interactions while building on common applications and proven mechanisms.

Disadvantages of a Tailored Solution

A tailored solution provides a balance between a packaged solution and an entirely customized one. This means that although it solves some problems associated with low-complexity solutions, it brings with it some of the issues associated with custom solutions, as follows:

- A tailored solution will involve a higher initial level of cost than simple solutions. This cost will be seen both in terms of the cost of software, hardware, and infrastructure, and in terms of the recruitment, retaining, and training of IT staff.

- The more specific a solution is to an organization, the less proven it may be. A solution including any level of customization is inherently more risky than one that employs only "vanilla" functionality.

- Although there are far more options available for integration, there is still no guarantee that a specific product will provide either the back-end integration or the sell-side integration you require. Lack of an appropriate integration mechanism may require you to purchase a third-party add-on or to create your own.

Strategies Supported by a Tailored Solution

Given the type and level of functionality available from a tailored solution, you can choose from the following strategy elements:

- Almost any direct, Web-based customer e-commerce interaction. Payment by common means such as credit card or purchase order via integrated services.

- Integration with common procurement and e-marketplace applications, providing personalized remote shopping and custom pricing.

- Customized order processing on a per customer basis, either locally within the e-commerce system or through existing order management applications.

- Value-added services for customers, including personalized advice and cross-selling of related products.

- Access to internal data sources that may be of use to customers, such as support databases.

As you can see, most things are possible using a tailored solution. The key is to select products that deliver the required functionality without too much customization.

Tailored Solution at Lamons Gasket

The requirements at Lamons Gasket led the senior management team to the conclusion that they needed a tailored solution based on standard applications. Given the company's requirements and its very restricted IT staff level (remember, it only has four IT staff), Lamons Gasket employed a third-party solutions provider to implement its system.

Important aspects of the system that was developed include the following:

- A new Web site that allows customers to search the company's catalog and place orders online. This includes specifying made-to-order or configurable items.

- Payment by credit card or by purchase order.

- Customer-specific pricing.

- Integration of the Web-based e-commerce system with an existing ERP system. Orders are transferred between the two automatically and error-prone manual processes are avoided.

- Direct submission of EDI-based orders into the ERP system without human intervention.

- Additional online customer services, such as order tracking and account maintenance facilities.

- A backbone of enterprise-class operating system and server software, including Microsoft Windows 2000, Microsoft SQL Server 2000, Microsoft Commerce Server 2000, and Microsoft BizTalk Server 2000.

Ken Frigo, Executive Vice President at Lamons Gasket, reflected on the benefits of these features, saying, "This should result in at least a 20 percent reduction in our customer service costs and has virtually eliminated the costs associated with data entry errors." This level of saving, together with an anticipated 15 to 25 percent increase in business, can quickly offset the cost of the development. Even the low end of the anticipated increase in business would yield $12 million per year.

Typical High-Complexity Supplier

As business requirements grow, so does the complexity of the solution that will be needed. The increase in requirements may be due to the sheer size and diversity of the organization, or it may be due to the complexity of its products or the markets in which it operates. Such organizations will typically require all of the functionality we have seen for a medium-complexity supplier but at an even higher level of flexibility and capacity. High-complexity suppliers may also have additional requirements, such as those that follow:

- The supplier will frequently form part of a complex automated supply chain or value chain. The success and profitability of the supplier and the other participants in the supply chain will depend on being able to add value as products and services pass along the chain. There is also a constant requirement to minimize cost and overhead associated with each stage of the chain. Both of these objectives require a very high level of integration, both with suppliers and customers.

- Increased complexity of products and services will require a higher degree of custom functionality to automate customer specification of, and interaction with, those products and services. This often includes configurable or build-to-order products or services.

- High-scale requirements such as significant order volumes or large numbers of products or services in the catalog(s).

- Increased complexity of markets (and of the organization itself) means that information on customer interactions is far more dispersed and variable. All of this must be collated to provide the sort of advanced analytics that allow an organization to become far more agile as it detects and responds to market changes.

- Multiple divisions and multiple business units, often with many instances of similar back-office applications such as ERP.

The increased requirements will tilt the balance between prebuilt functionality and customization in the solution. The result can be classified as a custom solution where a large amount of code or configuration is very specific to that organization and its business needs. Custom solutions share the attributes of tailored solutions, but these are more extreme, so the following is true:

- Although frequently based on packaged products, the amount of custom work is greater.

- More IT experience is required, both from solution providers and internally.

- More effort is required to ensure that nonfunctional requirements, such as high levels of availability, are achieved.

Again, the cost of such a solution will be progressively higher, but the payback comes in increased functionality, flexibility, and product differentiation.

Features of a Custom Solution

Custom solutions can take advantage of any products available to deliver particular features. Such solutions can encompass all the features available to a tailored solution, and in addition can deliver the following:

- Access to any automated procurement system or marketplace through customized software integration on the sell-side.

- Advanced analytical capabilities that can help detect trends early and thus help to position the business in a timely fashion. This may include getting out of unprofitable markets and getting into new ones. Such capabilities can help to detect subtle trends and opportunities for further marketing and selling.

- Complete integration with the back-end systems and business processes of the supplier organization. The costs required to create custom functionality to achieve this should be balanced against cost savings that may accrue from a reduction in manual effort to fill the gap left by incompatible systems.

- High levels of scalability, availability, and security as required by an organization.

In short, you can get as much functionality as you want, so long as you are willing to pay (and wait) for it.

Disadvantages of a Custom Solution

Custom solutions provide ultimate flexibility. Their disadvantages are mainly centered on available resources and change management, as follows:

- A custom solution will involve the highest level of cost. As with a tailored solution, this cost will be seen both in terms of the cost of software, hardware, and services, and also in terms of the recruitment, retaining, and training of IT staff.

- A custom solution will take longer to implement than a tailored solution. The more custom functionality required and the further that functionality moves away from the "sweet spots" of the underlying solutions, the longer it will take to develop and test.

- As the solution becomes increasingly customized and sophisticated, the risks associated with it will also increase. The world of IT is littered with examples of complex projects that were never completed because of the high levels of customization required and the inadequate level of planning and resources applied.

Strategies Supported by a Custom Solution

Given the type and level of functionality available from a custom solution, you can choose pretty much any strategy. Any strategy element listed for a tailored solution could be selected and implemented with a custom solution. In addition, custom solutions can open up the following possibilities:

- Complex product configuration capabilities. This may involve multiple user interactions or complex back-end processing to ensure that the product specified is represented correctly, and to provide custom pricing for the product. In many cases, this involves complex build-to-order scenarios.

- Advanced supply-chain integration so that information from your suppliers can be used to serve your customers. This may take the form of providing more accurate delivery time frames or pricing based on downstream supplier information. Such supply-chain integration also has benefits for your organization, as it can help you implement just-in-time ordering strategies that can further reduce prices for your customers.

Custom Solution at Equilon Lubricants

Because of the size and diversity of its customers, Equilon Lubricants wanted to employ a range of strategic elements. The level of functionality required led to a custom solution implemented with the help of several IT consulting partners.

Important aspects of the system developed include the following:

- Multichannel selling, providing access directly over the Web from automated procurement systems and e-marketplaces, which enables customer interactions from ERP systems or from standard PCs.

- Sell-side integration features that work with customers' ERP and procurement systems so that information about orders placed online is sent back to generate purchase orders within those customer ERP systems.

- The ability to publish custom catalogs for Equilon's customers that integrate with the customers' automated procurement systems. These systems can then interact directly with the e-commerce systems at Equilon, thereby reducing order-handling overheads.

- 24/7 access to all functionality.

- Flexible architecture that allows new customers to be added in one or two days. Previously, this took more than a week.

- A backbone of enterprise-class operating system and server software, including Microsoft Windows 2000, Microsoft Commerce Server 2000, and Microsoft BizTalk Server 2000.

As Larry Koenig, Director of eBusiness at Equilon Lubricants, reflects, "Using [the solution] we've deployed a flexible online catalog that can electronically trade with almost any buyer, both existing and new. We are in a unique position to offer our customers a value-added business relationship that can put us a step ahead of our competitors." Despite the complex requirements, the system was live less than 45 days after development started.

Summary: Appropriate Selection of Strategies and Solutions

In this chapter, we have discussed how strategies can be devised to deliver B2B e-commerce solutions for a wide range of suppliers, while maintaining differentiation and keeping to an appropriate budget. From a distance, such a feat seems like a circus act that requires the performer to keep a set of plates on poles spinning by constantly rushing between the poles and steadying each plate in turn. As you take on the role of the plate spinner, you need to be realistic about the number of plates you can spin. However, as you have seen, packaged solutions and development partners can help to spin many of these plates for you.

We have shown how some real companies have selected strategies to match their objectives and then selected solutions to match those strategies. We have described how the solutions themselves consist of a range of options that meet a variety of requirements—from simple to complex. We then showed how this typically maps out for suppliers with requirements ranging across low, medium, and high complexity.

The intention of this chapter was not to provide you with fixed strategies and solutions, as strategies and solutions will change over time. However, it should have equipped you with an understanding of the benefits, risks, and costs associated with different levels of functionality and given you an insight into the trade-offs involved in deciding what strategies to pursue based on this knowledge.

Implementing a Solution

Stop! You may be tempted to skip this chapter on the basis that it is probably full of techno-speak that will be irrelevant to you or even incomprehensible. Although we do discuss some important technologies and product types that you may use in your solution, this chapter is really about planning, not about precise selection of technologies or actual implementation and deployment. As the business decision maker, you will work with various departments within your organization, and possibly with external consultants as the strategies are mapped to precise solutions.

Our intention is to help you find your way through the selection processes that must occur and to demystify some of the key buzzwords that may be thrown around as the process unfolds. It is important for everyone involved in the process to exchange ideas and opinions clearly with as few misunderstandings as possible. To achieve this, you will not only need to ensure that the other stakeholders understand the business perspective, but you must also get to know a bit about their perspectives as well.

Once again, this chapter uses actual case studies, including real products and deployment information, as examples of how the assessment and selection process may unfold.

Doing It for Real

As you have read through this book, we have shown you the potential benefits and some of the pitfalls associated with enabling a supplier for business-to-business (B2B) e-commerce. You have seen some of the decisions made by other organizations, but now it's your turn. What about your own business? What are your requirements? Although we cannot answer these questions for you, we will certainly try to help you answer them for yourself.

Defining Objectives

As with the other organizations we have used as case studies, you must define your own objectives for selling electronically to your business customers.

What will you determine to be a success? Increased revenues? Reduced costs? Improved customer satisfaction ratings? Perhaps all of these and more. It is important to quantify your objectives and define how you are going to measure them. If you select increased revenue as one of your success criteria, you could measure it in a variety of ways:

- In terms of the absolute amount of incremental revenue brought in. For example, you want to earn an additional $500,000 in revenue from electronic sales in the first six months.

- In relative terms as part of existing or projected revenues. For example, you want B2B e-commerce revenues to form 10 percent of overall sales by the end of the first quarter.

- Some other form of figures. For example, 2 percent more revenue growth than anticipated before the B2B e-commerce initiative or a larger percentage of revenue from new or existing customers through electronic channels.

It is common to use a combination of success criteria, including both financial and nonfinancial criteria. The important thing is that the criteria must be measurable, which can in itself be a challenge. How do you measure customer satisfaction, for example?

When determining your objectives, it is important to take into account the market you are targeting. Are you looking to provide an electronic mechanism to integrate with those being put in place or considered by existing customers, or are you seeking new customers? Do your existing customers have the level of technology, budget, and intentions to take advantage of any strategies you put in place? There is no point in launching a major integration strategy unless your customers are willing to use it. If you are not sure, then some up-front investigation may be in order.

Your objectives will probably be a combination of quantifiable benefits *and* encapsulations of your aspirations for the solution. For example, you may target a revenue increase of 10 percent *and* want customers to be able to place orders without having to interact with a salesperson. Although it is more difficult to quantify and capture the latter type of objective, you should strive to do so, because defining such objectives is vital for a successful project. These functional objectives will form the basis of the requirements used when selecting a strategy and will be refined as the shape of the solution evolves.

When the project starts, you, or the appointed representative from the business, should adopt the role of stakeholder for the business and work with the IT management to ensure that the original objectives are still on course to be delivered. It is important that you perform a business "sanity check" at each stage of evolution. For example, at some stage, a detailed description may emerge of how a customer will place an order through a proposed remote shopping feature. You should have some experienced salespeople, or even customers themselves, review this process and check that it makes sense to the people involved in the business rather than the people involved in creating the technical solution.

Selecting Your Strategy

Once you have determined that enough of your customers will take advantage of B2B e-commerce or that it will drive significant new business, you must then determine what core mechanisms they will be using. Again, you need to do some research to discover whether your existing or potential customers already have electronic purchasing mechanisms in place. Do any existing systems dovetail with your own objectives, or do you require more in terms of differentiation or efficiency to achieve your objectives? Will existing and new customers adopt electronic purchasing methods in the near future?

Once you have the high-level objectives and information about the existing market context, you can start to determine appropriate strategies. As you select strategies, you should ask the following questions as objectively as you can:

- What will customers be able to do that they could not have done before?

- How does this add value to existing processes?

- How will you measure this?

- How does this contribute toward the overall objectives?

- How much (roughly) of the available budget will this strategy cost, and does this allow scope for other strategies that you may want to apply?

- How will it interact with any other strategies you may have determined (try to avoid creating a set of distinct and unrelated "islands" that do not deliver a consistent interaction with the customer)?

- What other consequences will the strategy have? This could be in terms of employees it might replace, or requirements from other parts of the business, such as the need to launch a marketing campaign to educate customers on the new initiative.

- How will your strategy, and the solutions you choose, scale and adapt to meet your anticipated levels of growth?

- How long will it take to implement your strategy?

- Can you implement your strategy in phases (and still achieve return on investment [ROI] in each phase)?

You might not like some of the answers to these questions, particularly if they indicate that your favored strategy will cost too much or take too long. This is why it is frequently worth looking at a phased approach. Bear in mind that the world of electronic commerce will be changing as you select your strategies and implement your solutions. The adoption of e-commerce strategies needs to be seen as an ongoing program, not a project. As the market changes, so must your strategies and the solutions that support them. Any strategy that takes too long to develop and roll out runs the risk of being overtaken by these movements. The agility and flexibility of your strategy and solutions are key factors in being able to deal with this rate of change.

Strategy selection is less like a shopping list and more like a recipe. It is important to blend the ingredients together in the right quantities and combinations to produce the desired results. You can taste and examine the dish as you go, adding seasoning or altering the blend until the combination is right.

Strategy Selection at Equilon Lubricants

When selecting appropriate strategies, Equilon Lubricants considered what its customers required at that point and what they would probably require in the immediate future. Equilon Lubricants identified that there were two core strategies required to integrate with its business customers:

- Direct integration between the customers' e-procurement systems and any solution implemented by Equilon Lubricants.

- Integration with e-marketplaces so that Equilon Lubricants' existing and new customers could access its products and services alongside those of other suppliers.

In addition to this distinction, it was recognized that within each category there would be multiple standards and protocols to support. This requires a flexible, multichannel solution to meet the needs of all customers.

Strategy Selection at Equilon Lubricants   *(continued)*

The solution that evolved from these strategies appears in Figure 5-1.

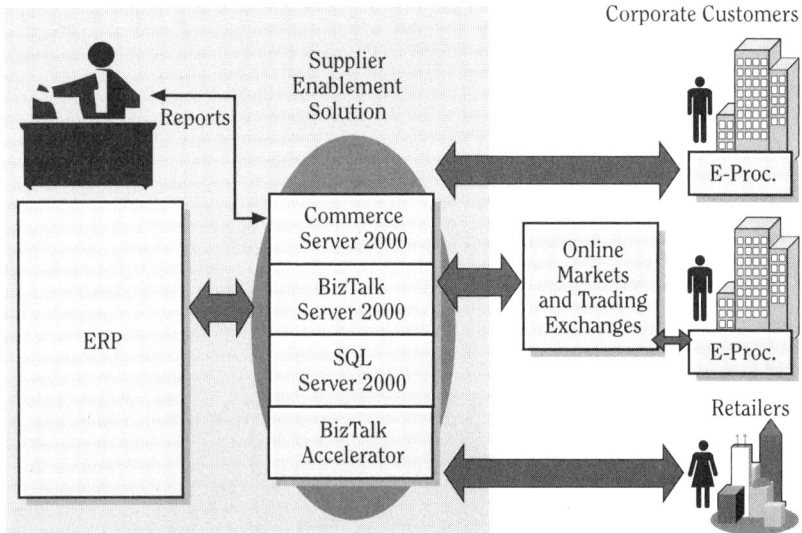

Figure 5-1.   *The solution for Equilon Lubricants allows it to integrate directly with customers' own e-procurement systems directly or through an e-marketplace. This enables customers to interact with Equilon Lubricants in their preferred way rather than being forced to use a specific mechanism.*

As you can see, the solution is based on the Microsoft Solution for Supplier Enablement including several of Microsoft's core enterprise server products: Microsoft Commerce Server 2000, Microsoft BizTalk Server 2000, and Microsoft SQL Server 2000. Such products are discussed at more length later in the chapter, but for now just be aware that Commerce Server provides the Web shopping and catalog functionality and BizTalk Server 2000 provides the ability to exchange business documents electronically using Extensible Markup Language (XML) and other formats such as electronic data interchange (EDI). In addition to the core server applications, the Microsoft Solution for Supplier Enablement also incorporates the Microsoft BizTalk Accelerator for Suppliers. This adds significant supplier-centric functionality and speeds up the process of integration with multiple sales channels.

The move from traditional EDI to an Internet-based strategy means that Equilon Lubricants can now rapidly integrate with new customers

(continued)

Strategy Selection at Equilon Lubricants   *(continued)*

and marketplaces. It also allows Equilon Lubricants to provide customers with additional value, including the following:

- "Live" catalogs that are tailored to customer requirements. The catalogs contain rich textual information and pictures of the product offerings.

- Remote shopping capability, either from the customer's own e-procurement system or an e-marketplace, allowing a collaborative and interactive experience.

- Rapid implementation of new integration mechanisms, as customers migrate from existing EDI-based systems to Internet-based solutions.

Although the strategies chosen by Equilon Lubricants included multiple channels and the ability to evolve in the face of change, those responsible for implementing the systems to support these strategies used simple building blocks to deliver the desired functionality.

Identifying Resources

The evolution and delivery of your strategies will depend on good input and advice from both the business stakeholders and the development team assigned to deliver the appropriate solution. If you are lucky, you may be blessed with a talented in-house IT team that already has experience delivering B2B e-commerce systems. If you are not so lucky, you may have to find resources elsewhere or adapt your plans to suit the resources available.

The number of IT staff available to implement and maintain the systems supporting the strategy will have a major impact on some of your decisions. If the appropriate skills are not available in-house, you may have to find the extra budget resources to hire or outsource them.

Internal Resources

Unless you are a very small company, you are likely to have some form of IT staff. It is vital that you engage your IT staff in any B2B e-commerce project because they will almost certainly inherit the responsibility for support and maintenance of the systems that result from the project. A large IT staff may be able to come up with the skills required to analyze, architect, and deliver the desired functionality. In this case, you should become involved as the business stakeholder in the internal project to ensure that the original vision is maintained or adjusted according to changing business requirements.

If your IT staff is small or does not have the appropriate skills, the project team may consist of three or more groups, as follows:

- Yourself, as the business stakeholder.

- One or more representatives of the internal IT department.

- One or more groups of third-party systems integrators, consultants, or vendors.

In this case, the internal IT staff can act as a bridge between the external technical specialists and the internal business specialists. Such IT staff should act as technical filters, judging the solutions proposed by the third parties. However, the IT staff should not, by themselves, represent your company, as direct input from the business side is critical to ensuring that the final system matches customer expectations.

If your company is small enough that you have no IT staff, you should turn to a service provider that can implement and host a solution on your behalf.

Consultants and Systems Integrators

If your IT staff has the numbers to address the project but lacks expertise in one or two areas, you may decide to bring in consultants. These consultants can range from technical specialists in areas such as e-commerce technologies and XML to e-business strategists who may help you define your overall strategy. If your organization intends to maintain and evolve its e-commerce capabilities into the future, you may use the expertise of such consultants, together with appropriate levels of training for your own staff, to ensure that your company gains the required skills during the initial project.

As the amount of development requiring outsourcing grows, you may turn to a specialized systems integrator or development house that can build or configure large parts of the system, or even all of it. The key issue in this case is selecting a systems integrator with a track record of delivering the type of solution you require or of helping similar companies in similar fields to successfully implement a B2B e-commerce strategy. To quote one satisfied user of such services, "[The]... consultants came in and provided project management services along with a proven set of techniques and methods, ensuring that the project would be successfully completed in a rapid and cost-effective manner."

As with any new vendor, you should do some investigation and obtain references from other satisfied customers if at all possible. If you decide to use a third party to develop the bulk of your system, you will need to determine how your company will maintain and support such a system.

Products and Product Vendors

If you have the people and technology skills in-house, but lack experience with a particular product or products, you may approach the product vendor for assistance. Most vendors have consultancy or professional service divisions and will usually provide some form of presales or postsales consultancy to help ensure that you apply their solutions appropriately.

When selecting products, you should be aware of the tendency of vendors to overstate the capabilities of their products. Try to satisfy yourself that someone on your side, either an internal IT employee or a third-party consultant, has sufficient knowledge to ask the right questions of the vendor regarding the functionality expected of its product(s) as part of your solution.

Service Providers

Finally, if your organization does not intend to host the solution itself, you will turn to some form of service provider. Do not make the selection of a service provider the last item on your list, to be sought after the solution development has begun. As with other consultants, you should select a service provider as part of your team and then have them work with you to help ensure that there is a smooth transition when the solution goes live.

Using External Consultants

As you have seen, external consultants can help a supplier to refine strategies and implement solutions. All of the suppliers used as case studies in this book took advantage of the services of a third-party consulting firm to help them select and implement their solutions.

Using External Consultants   *(continued)*

Given the nature of the solutions, these consultants are all Microsoft Certified Partners who can provide expertise in Microsoft products and solutions based on those products. Most product vendors run similar certification programs that can help you identify potential partners with the necessary skills and track record.

TCS and Cactus Communications Internet

TCS was able to implement its solution in 37 days with the help of Cactus Communications Internet, a Microsoft Gold Certified Partner for e-commerce solutions. Here are some of the ways in which Cactus helped TCS achieve that:

- It was able to identify and deliver a targeted solution (the Microsoft Solution for Supplier Enablement in this case) that addresses TCS's requirements, and also its budget.

- It used a standard process for specifying and delivering the solution, based on the Microsoft Solutions Framework (MSF). This is just one embodiment of the experience and track record that such a consultancy organization can bring to bear.

- Cactus' experience with the technology solution involved meant that there was no learning curve required before the project could start. The staff at TCS could learn alongside the consultants as the system was designed and developed.

The solution not only delivered what was needed by the business now, but allowed plenty of scope for future growth, according to Jeff Odom, President of TCS Corporate Services:

> *While Cactus was able to design a powerful e-commerce system for our immediate needs, what's perhaps more important is where this system puts us in terms of our market. We think it puts us far ahead of any of our competitors, and if our customers want totally integrated suppliers, we're going to make it to a lot more top-tier lists.*

(continued)

Using External Consultants   *(continued)*

Equilon Lubricants and CGE&Y

Cap Gemini Ernst and Young (CGE&Y), together with Microsoft Consultancy Services (MCS), helped Equilon Lubricants to deliver their B2B e-commerce strategies in six weeks. CGE&Y were involved in all stages of the business transformation:

- CGE&Y worked with Equilon Lubricants to identify the core business processes required to improve customer satisfaction and increase sales.

- Delivery of an early proof of concept implementation showed that the system was capable of handling all of the various complex business rules required by the system.

- Iterative development allowed the solution to be rolled out rapidly.

Once again, the delivered solution could not have been achieved in the timescale without the product and e-commerce experts provided by third party consultants.

Enabling Technologies

When you start meeting with your IT staff, product vendors, and systems integrators, a variety of diagrams will be drawn showing how your organization will interact with your customers and suppliers. These diagrams will frequently be drawn from a technical perspective and will consist of boxes and lines annotated with technology and product names such as cXML, xCBL, HTTP, OCI, and BizTalk. Most technical terms and acronyms are as impenetrable to nontechnical people as Celtic runes or Sanskrit are to the authors of this book. Regardless of your technical knowledge, it is important that you as the business stakeholder, ask this important question: "How does this product, technology, or solution help to deliver on the objectives we have agreed on?" In this section, we will provide answers to that question based on common technologies and products typically used in B2B e-commerce solutions. Hopefully, this will give you the ability to decipher at least some of the language. Moreover, you should be able to validate the story from the technical experts and product vendors against that which we describe here.

Web Technologies

As we stated in *Chapter 1, "The Role of Suppliers in Business-to-Business E-Commerce,"* the Internet is the great driver for electronic trade. If we compare the Information Revolution with previous business revolutions, the Internet is the information equivalent of the physical transportation network in that it transports data from organization to organization. The delivery mechanisms are precise—they can deliver information and services from a server halfway around the world directly to the Web browser on a PC. If you book and take a scheduled airline flight to your favorite vacation spot, you will probably not stop to marvel at the level of engineering, organization, and skill required to transport you comfortably and safely from your departure gate to your destination. In the same way, it is easy to forget how much effort has gone into making access to those many Internet-based applications and sources of information as simple as clicking a mouse button.

The use of Web technologies has the potential to make your B2B e-commerce integration perform as seamlessly as that mouse click. If you are delivering product or catalog information to a person sitting in front of a Web browser, the natural way to deliver that information is as Hypertext Markup Language (HTML). Almost all of the information you see as you use the Web is surrounded by HTML instructions that tell your Web browser how to display that information (images, tables, lists, and so on).

Information Age Transportation

As stated earlier, the Internet serves as the railroad tracks linking organizations around the globe. However, you still need a train to run on those tracks, picking up and delivering passengers and freight. In Web terms, this transportation is performed by the Hypertext Transfer Protocol (HTTP). As you can infer from its name, it is designed to carry information wrapped up in HTML. HTTP uses the reliable "railroad tracks" of the Internet to carry requests from your Web browser to distant servers and to return the information you require.

At this point, you may be thinking "So what? Why are they talking about Web pages? I want to integrate my applications with those of my trading partners." Bear with us as we explain. HTTP has become one of the major building blocks for B2B e-commerce because the Web is everywhere. Millions of companies around the world have Web sites, and every interaction with those Web sites takes place over HTTP. Because of its ubiquity, HTTP has the ability to pass through Internet security barriers (commonly termed *firewalls*) that protect organizations from some of the less savory characters that roam the

Internet. Another ubiquitous way of transporting data used on the Internet is e-mail. Web and e-mail traffic form the lifeblood of the Internet, so they generally pass freely into and out of organizations.

You can compare these mechanisms to the way in which telephones (analogous to HTTP) and postal services (analogous to e-mail) are used by businesses to communicate with each other in the physical world. Businesses will use the telephone and postal services to exchange goods and information with both customers and suppliers. In the case of B2B interactions, a certain level of automation may already be in place using these ways of exchanging data. A phone line may be used to carry a fax so that data exchange does not rely on a person relaying the order by voice. Similarly, an incoming purchase order may be scanned into a system that uses character recognition to obviate the need for its contents to be retyped. In the same way, if you want to exchange information or services directly between your systems and those of your customers, you can use the ubiquitous services of HTTP and e-mail.

Information Age Information

One major issue remains. When sending product information to a customer browsing your online catalog with a Web browser, you will send that information as HTML. However, if you are sending the same information directly to another system, rather than a Web browser, it probably does not want to be told how to *display* the information. Rather, it wants to know how each piece of information relates to the information around it and what the overall purpose of that information is. For example, the receiving application must be told that the information represents a purchase order. Take the example of an order from one of your customers. When viewing it on a Web page, it may be presented as a table. Each row in the table contains a description of the item, the quantity requested, an item identification number, the unit price, and so on. At the top of each column, there is a label telling you what the contents of the column mean (for example, the label *Quantity* means that the numbers in that column indicate how many of a particular item are being requested). This is relatively easy for you to understand because the Web browser will have formatted the information into a table, as instructed by the HTML, and your brain will be able to make the association between the column label and the numbers in that column. You will also intuitively understand how a quantity value relates to the row in which it resides (in other words, if the row has an item description of "gold-plated widgets," you will know that the quantity value of 500 on the same row means your customer is about to order 500 gold-plated widgets).

Unfortunately, machines and applications are not yet able to make such intuitive leaps. They must be told precisely how each piece of information relates to the others around it. This is where XML comes in. Although it looks superficially like HTML, the purpose of XML is to describe the context of the data itself, rather than how to display it. Using XML, an application can produce a description of, say, a purchase order that can be easily processed and understood by another application.

XML is another core building block used for Internet-based B2B e-commerce. It can be easily carried over the Internet by HTTP and e-mail, giving it almost universal access to customer and supplier companies around the globe. Its machine-readable nature means that it is ideal for reducing the amount of human intervention required in business processes. Its complete flexibility means that it can be applied in any business domain you could care to mention. In addition to being machine-readable, it is actually a descriptive, text-based language, so humans stand a chance of being able to understand it, if they care to do so.

Note   The human-readable nature of XML is in contrast to most EDI systems. (You may recall that we have talked about EDI before as providing one of the first means of exchanging business data electronically between businesses.) EDI formats are usually heavily encoded and can only really be interpreted by specialized software and EDI specialists. Having said that, it is not realistic to expect to replace most existing EDI systems with XML-based solutions. Therefore, you should ensure that the solution you choose is able to integrate with existing EDI systems used by your customers.

Now that you have some background on XML, HTTP, and e-mail, we can move on to examine how they can be applied to deliver effective B2B e-commerce.

XML Dialects

Although XML is a great enabler for e-commerce, it is not without its faults. We find that the following statement sums this up rather succinctly: The great advantage of XML is its extreme flexibility—it can be adapted and applied in an infinite variety of ways. The great disadvantage of XML is its extreme flexibility—it can be adapted and applied in an infinite variety of ways.

No, you didn't read that incorrectly. There is a real danger that XML's great strength, its flexibility, can actually work against it. The basics of XML are standardized through a body called the World Wide Web Consortium (W3C; *www.w3c.org*). However, this only defines how you create your own information descriptions (or *tags*). The XML standard does not define a way of describing a purchase order or invoice; it simply provides a neat way of doing so. The idea is that somebody who knows about the information in question, be it purchase orders or orchestral symphonies, can use XML to define his or her own set of tags that are specific to that subject.

As you may expect, the result has been organized chaos. In some academic areas, such as mathematics or chemistry, people have collaborated (with only a bit of dissent) to produce common tag sets, or XML dialects, that can be used to describe their own subject area. In other areas, where the financial stakes are far higher, there has been a proliferation of languages from technology vendors and industry consortia as each seeks to gain (and lock in) customers. (If you wish to see the effects of this explosion yourself, visit the XML Cover pages at *http://www.oasis-open.org/cover* and look at the list of potential "Applications.")

Sadly, B2B e-commerce is one area in which such a proliferation has taken place. Many different XML-based e-commerce dialects have arisen. Thankfully, the market is a fairly Darwinian environment, meaning that only a few have really survived and prospered, among which are Commerce XML (cXML) and the XML Common Business Library (xCBL), together with various industry-specific dialects. However, the existence of any more than one dialect to describe the business documents you will need to create or process means that you will need flexible, well-designed systems to cope with such variety. One saving grace in this area is the eXtensible Stylesheet Language for Transformation (XSLT). XSLT is another W3C standard that allows a suitably equipped tool or developer to define how a document in one XML dialect can be converted (or transformed) into a different XML dialect.

Web Services

The Web uses common standards to allow Web browsers and Web servers from different vendors to work together. You do not have to start a Netscape Web browser to retrieve Web pages from a Netscape Web server any more than you have to use a Microsoft Web browser to retrieve Web pages from a Microsoft Web server. It is the platform-agnostic nature of the Web that has allowed it to grow and flourish.

In B2B terms, the Web is only part of the equation. Being able to fetch HTML pages is fine for the searching and ordering parts of remote shopping. However, what happens when the order that the customer has created needs to be passed back to the customer's own purchasing system? Well, you can wrap the order information in the appropriate form of XML and deliver it back to that application. This is fine as far as it goes, but what we have just described is a fairly limited exchange of information. If we are really going to integrate with the business processes of our varied customers and suppliers, we need more.

Applying Web Services

The concept of Web services is quite simple. If you are developing a Web-based application that requires credit card processing, you have the following choices:

- Invest the time and effort in creating and maintaining your own credit card processing software.

- Buy credit card processing software that you can install as part of your solution.

- Delegate all of your credit card processing to a third party.

It is this third option that is of the most interest for many e-business solutions. Most businesses (both large and small) do not normally want the overhead of processing credit card transactions themselves. In response to this, various companies offer credit card processing services across the Internet that can be used by anyone developing a Web-based application. This reduces the complexity of such an application and also reduces the up-front cost, because the charge for the credit card processing service is generally based on the number of transactions processed.

Companies that provide Web services will define the types of service they provide, what is required for you to take advantage of those services, and what you will get in return. In the case of credit card processing, you will have to provide them with the card number, the cardholder's name, the expiration date, and the amount to be debited (over a secure connection, of course). The processing company will return success or failure information, such as an authorization code, back to your application across the Internet. Your application can then use this information to proceed with the customer's transaction.

(continued)

Applying Web Services   *(continued)*

Web services address various business needs and provide an infrastructure for Web-based applications. Some examples are listed next:

- **Payment.** If payment for goods or services is by credit card or electronic transfer, an e-commerce application must process the payment. Third-party Web services for payment processing allow the application to delegate the mechanisms for such processing to a specialist clearinghouse.

- **Authentication.** The correct identification of customers is vital for personalization and payment. By using a third-party Web service for authentication, customers can take their digital identity with them without having to authenticate themselves to your application over and over again, making it easier to use.

- **Logistics.** Any physical products that you sell will need to be shipped to your customers. If the shipping company offers the ability to make such arrangements available through a Web service, this can form a seamless part of your application.

- **Credit.** A third party can act as a credit broker to add further value to the flow of transactions between two parties. Offering this as a Web service makes it easier for both parties to build it into their applications.

- **Business registries.** When seeking new customers and suppliers, organizations can make use of third-party registries compiled by marketplaces or industry consortia. Web services provide an ideal mechanism for making this information available. A variety of applications can use these services to make it easier to find and integrate with new business partners and additional Web services.

- **Collaboration.** Integration is not just about the flow of goods and services, but also about the sharing of ideas and information. Collaborative tools can be offered as Web services, allowing partners to easily import them into new or existing applications and processes.

- **Conversion.** Various Web service–based conversion mechanisms are available, providing everything from currency rate conversion to language translation.

Applying Web Services   *(continued)*

This list is not exhaustive, but it should give you an idea of the diverse nature of Web services and some of the ways in which they can add value to an application. In each case, they remove the need for the application development team to have knowledge of that specific area of business or technology. In return for this development and maintenance benefit, you will usually pay a fee to use the Web service.

The application development model of Web services parallels that of component software that has been prevalent over the last few years. In both cases, application logic takes advantage of previously offered third-party functionality. The rise of component software has created a market in third-party components and in application builder tools. In the same way, such markets and tools are appearing in the Web services arena, making it easier and quicker to develop applications based around Web services.

The Web service framework provides access to more sophisticated and complex Web-based services and information. At the time of writing this book, the Web services platform provides the following:

- A description of the business functions that a particular Web service offers, such as "process payment" or "convert currency." This description must be provided in a form that makes it easy for your B2B e-commerce application to understand and use those functions. The Web Services Description Language (WSDL) provides a description of the functions offered by a service using a specially developed dialect of XML, making it easy for your e-commerce application to process and understand it. The WSDL service description also contains the Web address where the associated Web service can be found.

- A way of specifying which business function you want to use and passing it the associated business information, such as the line items in the purchase order. For all their benefits, HTTP and e-mail were only intended to carry ordinary documents. What is needed here is something a bit smarter. The Simple Object Access Protocol (SOAP) provides this extra intelligence. SOAP uses HTTP or e-mail to pass business messages, but it takes care of the higher level concerns such as specifying which business function to use and delivering the correct business information for that function.

- A way of finding all of this information. In the past, system developers would be confronted with bookcases full of manuals that described how particular software applications could be used. Although these paper manuals have given way to electronic versions, they still rely on developers reading and understanding the documentation before they can use the functionality. Because Web services bring their own description in the form of WSDL, and that description also contains location information about that specific Web service, passing the information around in a "manual" will simply not work. The Universal Description, Discovery, and Integration (UDDI) protocol provides a way to store and access information about Web services in their native environment, online. The overall interaction is shown in Figure 5-2.

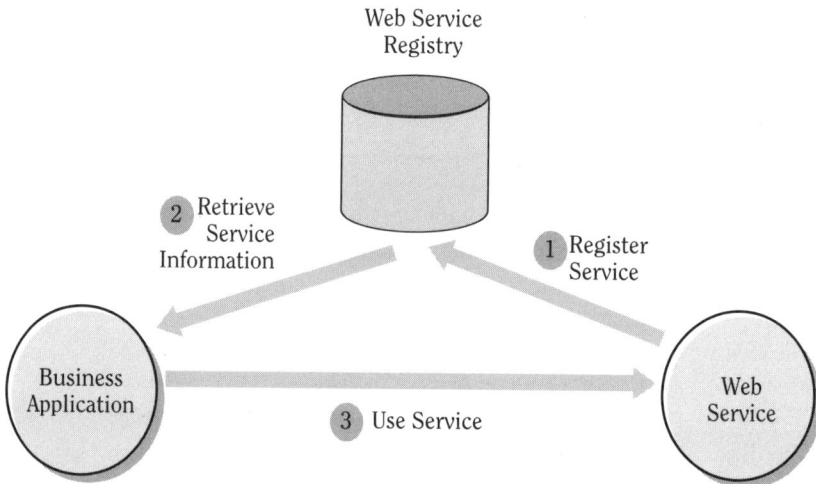

Figure 5-2.   *A Web service will register its information in a registry. This information can be found and retrieved by applications that wish to use the Web service.*

The important thing here is that these technologies allow us to start emulating real-world business practices. UDDI allows you to look up a service in multiple ways. If you know the precise service you need, you can identify it directly, much in the way you would look up the telephone number of a known business partner in the regular phone directory, commonly called the white pages. Alternatively, if you wanted to find all the couriers in your area, you would look in a phone directory that categorizes its entries based on what they provide, commonly called the yellow pages. UDDI provides this type of yellow pages service so that you can discover new suppliers of the type of Web service you want to use. In addition to this, UDDI provides a "green pages" service that allows you to search for a particular Web service based on information about the style of interaction(s) it supports.

Microsoft Passport as an Example Web Service

Microsoft Passport is widely regarded as one of the first realistic Web services in production on the Internet. The problem that Passport addresses is that Web users frequently have to create new identities and profiles at a variety of different Web sites and online services. This becomes tiresome and difficult to manage after a while, as people frequently forget their different user IDs and passwords. This situation is also somewhat insecure and inconsistent, as a user's details and preferences are stored in many places across the Web.

With Passport, users do not have to create a different identity for every new site they visit or Web application they interact with. A participating site will use the Passport Web Service to authenticate users. Users will provide their e-mail address and their Passport password, and the Passport Web Service will provide confirmation that the authentication was successful. The Web application can then access all, some, or none of the users' profile information, depending on settings decided by the users themselves. Shared profile information means that users do not have to set up that profile information with every Web application, thus making things easier once again. The associated Passport wallet functionality allows Passport-enabled applications to request payment information from the Passport service. Again, this means less typing for users, and—more important—they retain control over their information because it is linked to their Passport identity.

The original Passport service has been available for some time and uses some of the Web service mechanisms outlined in the main body of this chapter. The replacement for Passport—the Microsoft .NET My Services—uses even more core Web service standards to deliver additional power and convenience.

For more information on Passport, see *http://www.microsoft.com/passport*. For more information on the .NET My Services, see *http://www.microsoft.com/net*.

Now that you understand the frameworks within which your B2B e-commerce application will likely be operating, we can examine some of the products that make it easier to work in this environment.

Enterprise Software Platforms

By now, you know the basic technology story underpinning Internet-based B2B e-commerce. Add this to your business requirements and we can begin to build a clear picture of the type of software solution that can help to deliver on your objectives. It goes without saying that the solution will need to deliver a certain level of flexibility, reliability, and scalability, as well as the required functionality. This is true, regardless of whether the software is implemented within your company or hosted by a third party, and whether you are a big company or a small one. There is no point in committing yourself to an e-commerce strategy that will form the basis of a sizable chunk of your revenue if you then build the solution based on an inadequate software foundation.

The general term for such quality products and platforms is *enterprise servers*. We can roughly categorize the enterprise servers used in B2B e-commerce solutions into three main types, as follows:

- **Database servers.** Information, or data, is the lifeblood of any organization. Whether it is customer contact information, product details, sales figures, or the contents of a single purchase order, the management of and access to that data is vital to the proper working of the organization. Because of this, most organizations already have some form of data storage, ranging from spreadsheets and handheld personal organizers to specialized database systems that can hold years' worth of sales data for global organizations. Enterprise class database servers, such as Microsoft SQL Server and Oracle, are intended for the storage and retrieval of enterprise data. Such products can be judged on capacity, speed of access, and additional functionality. Because this data forms the core of your online operations, you will want to ensure that the database server you choose "plays well with others," in that it is well supported by other servers and tools that will be used to build the solution.

- **Commerce servers.** A commerce server is, as the name would suggest, targeted at building e-commerce sites. Some commerce servers are largely targeted at business-to-consumer (B2C) e-commerce, whereas others provide both B2C and B2B capabilities. The core functionality of commerce servers includes the creation of the Web site itself, catalog management, shopping cart functionality, the processing of orders, and other customer-oriented interactions, such as personalization and marketing.

- **Integration servers.** The widespread enthusiasm and uptake of XML and Web data transport mechanisms has seen the arrival of a new breed of integration servers. These servers are primarily based on the exchange of XML messages over various standard transport mechanisms such as HTTP or SOAP. Integration servers provide the ability to manipulate, route, transform, and propagate XML-based business messages and documents. An organization might need one or more integration servers, depending on the size of the organization. Business messages will be sent between integration servers in your organization and those in other organizations until they reach their destination. Integration servers tend to provide a high level of reliability when it comes to message delivery (in other words, it will either definitely get there or definitely be returned; it will not get "lost in the mail").

Based on the sort of requirements for supplier systems explored in *Chapter 4, "Business Strategies and Solutions,"* we will now discuss how these types of enterprise servers could be used as part of your solution.

Making Products and Services Available

Suppliers already have the catalog information, namely product and pricing, required by their customers. The challenge is to make that information available in a flexible way to suit customer requirements.

By examining successful e-commerce implementations, catalog storage and manipulation responsibilities can be delegated to those servers that perform each task the best. This means that ideally the product information should be stored in a database server, managed by a commerce server, and transformed and delivered by an integration server.

Many suppliers will have much of their existing product and pricing information stored in database servers. If the information is not stored in such a way, the commerce server's catalog management facilities should make it relatively easy to import from other sources.

Although database servers provide the raw capability for holding and exporting catalog information, commerce servers provide specific functionality to help build and maintain an online catalog that wraps around such raw data storage. Commerce servers also provide simple ways of publishing catalog information as HTML pages that customers can access over the Web, possibly as part of a remote shopping solution. The same type of functionality can also be used to provide rudimentary XML-based publishing, and hence support for multiple sales channels.

The role played by integration servers in catalog publication is the conversion of internal data into different data formats for different customers. Integration servers are the key to supporting multiple sales channels, not only because they can handle multiple XML dialects and other formats, but also because they support multiple transport mechanisms. Combined with a commerce server, this delivers the underlying support for all of the different types of customer interactions you will require as part of your various strategies.

All commerce servers provide basic online shopping capabilities such as virtual shopping carts. Most are also able to adapt the published information to particular customers so that they receive custom catalogs and custom pricing. Additional sell-side integration can be achieved through the use of pipelines that allow the buying process or the processing of orders to be customized by adding new functionality as an additional or tailored stage of the pipeline, as shown in Figure 5-3.

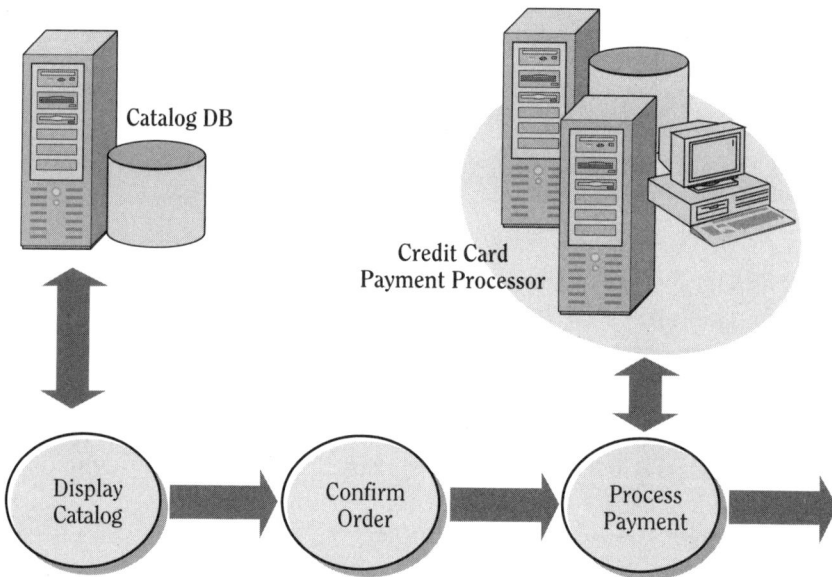

Figure 5-3.   *Commerce servers employ pipelines that combine simple building blocks to deliver a sophisticated service. Each building block can be replaced without affecting the others. For example, the step labeled Process Payment is shown to interact with a credit card payment processing system. This step could easily be replaced by one that processes purchase orders for corporate customers. Additional steps can also be inserted at any point to provide extra processing.*

The pipeline model is used to allow you to customize some of the interactions with users, such as the sequence of steps followed when they are browsing your catalog and selecting items as part of a remote shopping session. Once the remote shopping session is complete, the order information can be passed to an integration server to be transformed into the appropriate format and delivered back to the customer's system.

Order Management

Orders can be received from a customer either by a commerce server or by an integration server, depending on the style of the solution. Using an integration server, orders from customers can be processed and forwarded to the appropriate internal systems without human intervention. If a customer or supplier uses a different dialect of XML to describe a business document, then the integration server provides a convenient location where you can transform that document into your own XML dialect.

Once the order has been appropriately transformed, the integration server can then submit the order for further processing by the business systems. This may involve delivering it to an enterprise resource planning (ERP) system or processing it further by a pipeline on the commerce server. Part of the order processing will log the details in a database server for subsequent reference, audit, and business intelligence purposes.

Once the order has been submitted, customers may wish to examine its progress. This will involve the use of an integration server and commerce server to extract the progress information from an ERP system or database server and then convert it into the appropriate format before sending it on to the customer's application.

The automated receipt and handling of an order will require various messages to be exchanged with the customer's application. This sequence of message exchange forms part of a business process that spans from the customer's applications to yours and must be managed to provide seamless integration. This choreography or orchestration of business messages includes acknowledgment of messages and error handling. The best integration servers will allow you to define your business processes and execute them. This simplifies the mechanism for setting up a B2B e-commerce partnership by allowing partners to agree on predefined automated business processes using standard message formats.

Business Intelligence

One of the commonly required functions for B2B e-commerce solutions that database servers can provide is business intelligence. The ability to use advanced analytical techniques to spot trends in huge quantities of data can help to ensure that your ongoing business decisions are soundly based and can be proactive, rather than reactive.

In addition to the analysis of data stored in databases, the most useful commerce servers will come with additional functionality that allows you to gather and analyze sales and product information. This type of analysis complements the business intelligence functionality provided by database servers.

Integration with Existing Systems

To achieve real benefits in terms of automating business processes, the new e-commerce system must be able to integrate with existing systems, such as ERP systems. Commerce servers will generally provide some integration with back-end systems, whether that is with your internal ERP or finance systems or direct communication with your own suppliers' systems.

The inherent transformation capabilities of integration servers make them powerful tools for back-end integration as well as sell-side integration. The integration server may be used by the commerce server to transform business documents conforming to its own data format into those formats required by back office applications such as an ERP system. The business process orchestration capabilities of integration servers can also be used to choreograph exchanges with internal systems.

Microsoft BizTalk Server 2000

Microsoft BizTalk Server 2000 is an example of an integration server that enables you to rapidly build and deploy integrated business processes, both within your organization and with your trading partners. The product allows you to integrate with many and varied partner systems in the following ways:

- **Messaging and delivery.** BizTalk Server allows you to select and define message formats and transport mechanisms used

---

Microsoft BizTalk Server 2000   *(continued)*

to exchange messages with business partners. For example, the BizTalk Messaging Manager allows graphical selection of exchange mechanisms and agreements between trading partners. The server itself supports multiple common transport mechanisms to aid integration.

- **Mapping and transformation.** BizTalk Server has powerful transformation capabilities that allow you to exchange business information in the correct format for your business partners. The BizTalk Mapper tool allows you to select, apply, and customize transformations that convert between your document formats and those of your trading partners. This is not limited to XML documents, as BizTalk Server can handle EDI documents and other forms of application-specific files, translating between those formats and XML where necessary. The BizTalk Editor allows you to create XML versions of your own business documents for easier processing.

- **Orchestration and business process flow.** Using BizTalk Server, you can rapidly integrate business processes with trading partners. For example, the BizTalk Orchestration Designer tool allows you to model business process interactions visually and then helps you translate this model into an appropriate solution.

BizTalk Server takes advantage of common standards, such as the BizTalk Framework, which is an industry framework for reliable document exchange and routing. Naturally, all of its XML processing and document transportation is based on Internet and Web standards.

As you can see, using such a server as part of your solution goes a long way toward integrating with most of your trading partners and their business processes.

The only caveat relating to integration servers is to ensure that the server you choose will integrate and interoperate easily with the products, standards, and e-marketplaces used by your customers. You

(continued)

Microsoft BizTalk Server 2000   *(continued)*

should therefore think about two things when selecting an integration server. First, you should try to ensure that the integration server you choose supports as many common standards as possible. Second, a high degree of flexibility and "plugability" is required from the integration server. Not every customer application will be catered for by out-of-the-box functionality. Indeed, a considerable amount of configuration may be required to apply the adapters provided with the integration server to your specific requirements. Also, new standards are appearing on a regular basis, so your integration server should be able to evolve to meet your solution requirements. This flexibility should be embodied in tools that allow you to quickly and easily create and configure the adapters provided or enabled by the integration server.

Applying Enterprise Servers

Figure 5-4 shows the overall objective. The solution must act as a gateway between internal data and services and external customers. The correct combination of servers will allow business processes to flow between your organization and those of your customers in an efficient and manageable way.

By using enterprise servers that build on the technology discussed earlier, you can deliver solutions much faster and to a higher level of quality than you could if you do not include them in your solution. Such servers provide the basis for almost all recent successful e-commerce solutions.

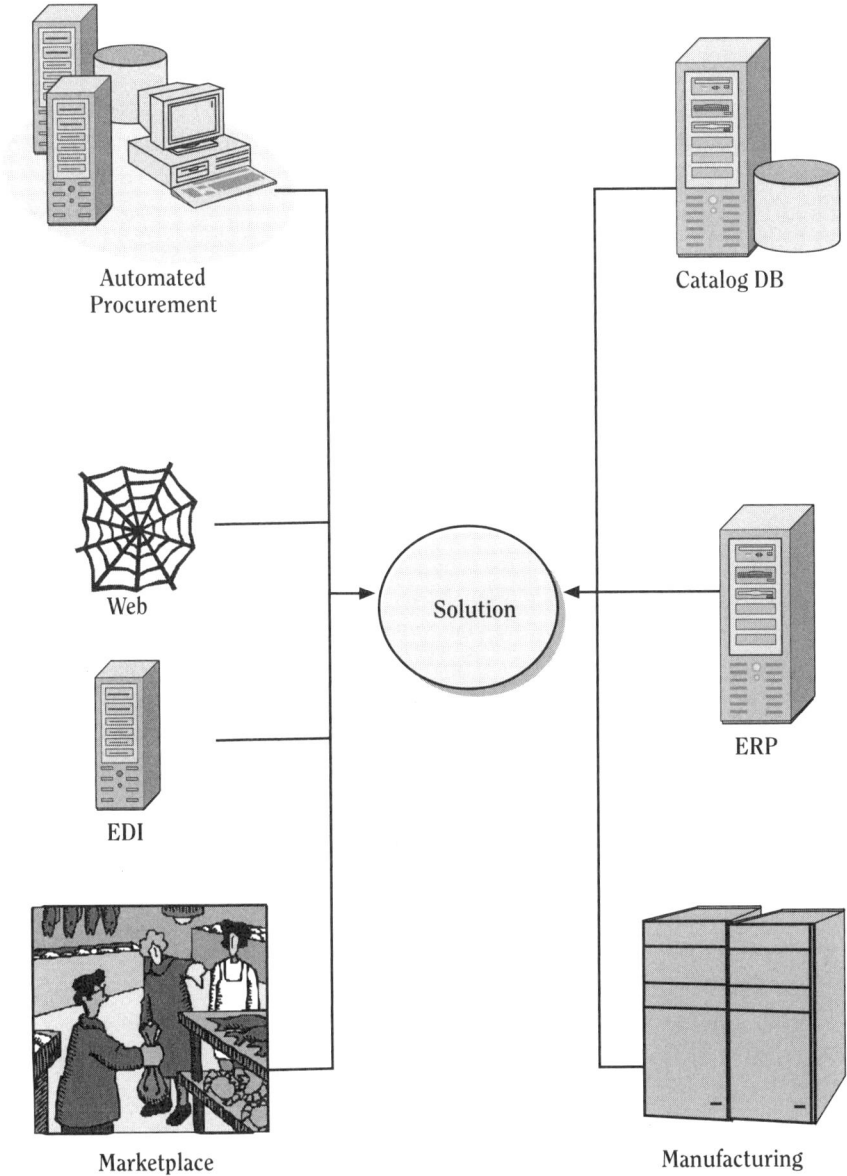

Figure 5-4. *The appropriate combination of servers can provide a solution that integrates with various types of customer application and also with multiple internal applications.*

Applying Enterprise Servers at MarkMaster

MarkMaster and its consultants used the core enterprise servers of the Microsoft Solution for Supplier Enablement in the following ways, serving as the foundation of their solution:

- **Making products available.** Microsoft Commerce Server 2000 exposes the product catalogs to direct Web users and provides them with shopping cart functionality, together with other common Web-based shopping features. Microsoft SQL Server 2000 is used to store the underlying product data. BizTalk Server 2000 is used to deliver and transform the product information directly to the purchasing applications at MarkMaster's customers.

- **Order management.** Microsoft BizTalk Server 2000 plays a key role in the integration with automated procurement systems and marketplaces used by large customers. These systems send business documents, such as purchase orders, to be processed by the system without direct human intervention. Received orders are transformed into MarkMaster's preferred format using BizTalk Server 2000, managed by Commerce Server 2000, and stored using SQL Server 2000.

- **Business intelligence.** SQL Server 2000 provides the business intelligence engine delivered as part of the solution, and Commerce Server 2000 provides the reporting and analysis tools.

Figure 5-5 gives an overview of how enterprise servers were used at MarkMaster. The Microsoft Solution for Supplier Enablement was applied to take advantage of the "sweet spots" of each server, thereby giving MarkMaster a better chance of achieving its objectives. By choosing such an integrated solution, based on one product family, MarkMaster could ensure that the different underlying products would work together well. Just as important, an integrated solution can be implemented and supported as one offering, rather than many separate products. The implementation partner (Compaq Global Services) was able to obtain complete training and support for the entire solution, accelerating the deployment and ensuring the success of the project.

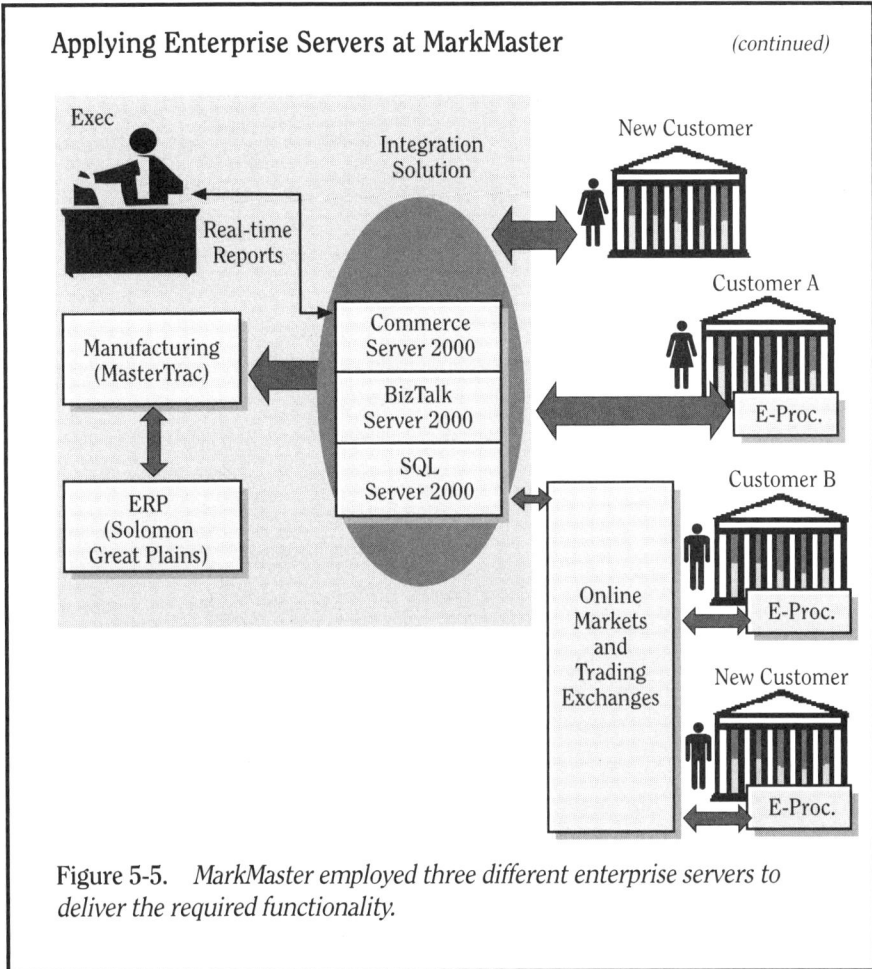

Figure 5-5. *MarkMaster employed three different enterprise servers to deliver the required functionality.*

E-Commerce Packages and Solutions

As you may have gathered by now, the world of e-commerce is rapidly changing and evolving. Today's state-of-the-art e-commerce system is as likely to be overtaken by a shift in business models, as it is a new wave of technology. As new markets and ways of working appear, vendors emerge to fill particular niches and explore the bounds of each new business model.

Take automated procurement systems as an example. The remote shopping functionality we described earlier in this book was not part of the first wave of automated procurement systems three to four years ago. Given this, one option for buyers was to import all the suppliers' catalog information a system required. Another option would have been to "fake" the remote shopping part as an entirely separate process for employees, effectively the same as B2C Web-based shopping but with purchase order numbers instead of credit card numbers. This would be done by having the supplier provide a separate Web site that the employees would interact with outside of the control of their procurement systems—not a great story for the buyer. In response to such issues, the early implementers of such systems created service-based offerings to deliver integrated solutions for a limited set of customers and suppliers. Soon after this happened, one or more small vendors, possibly even the consultants who implemented the custom systems for buyers, began developing and promoting products that addressed this particular niche. This happened with the appearance of such functionality as Ariba's PunchOut and Commerce One's RoundTrip.

Remote Shopping at TCS

As part of its solution, TCS has used the remote shopping facilities delivered as part of the Microsoft Solution for Supplier Enablement (see sidebar "The Accelerated Solution") to integrate with customer applications. Customers can use e-procurement systems or e-marketplaces to find TCS's product offerings using a "punch-out" mechanism.

A potential buyer can view an initial description of a TCS product—a laser printer, for example—and then click on that item to be transferred directly to a personalized view of the TCS Web site, created and managed by Commerce Server 2000. The customer can then select product options as appropriate. Once all the parameters for the product are chosen, the buyer is transferred back to the e-marketplace site for financial completion of the transaction. This involves the delivery of the order information back to the customer's system so that it can be checked and approved within the rules of its procurement system. The customer system will then automatically submit the purchase order to TCS's systems, where it will be received and processed by the combination of BizTalk and Commerce Server, and then delivered to back-end accounting and fulfillment systems automatically.

This system allows TCS to differentiate itself from other suppliers in this market while facilitating targeted marketing and other ways to improve customer service.

Inevitably, if particular areas of functionality appeal to the wider market, support for this functionality will begin to appear in mainstream commerce servers in the form of prebuilt adapters that can speed integration with buyers or suppliers who already use that functionality. These adapters are frequently built in collaboration with the small vendors who wish to see the market for their technology solutions grow. The large vendors will incorporate this technology into their overall enterprise solution, providing customers with an integrated solution from a name they know and trust and whose software they are already using.

With or without third-party technology, large vendors who identify needs from their customers have started to align their products into solution sets, where they concentrate less on selling individual enterprise servers and more on selling a whole solution. Like small vendors, the large vendors can build solution sets based around tried and tested combinations used by early adopters in the market who use their products. Specifically targeted e-commerce solutions are appearing for B2B e-commerce, supply chains, automated procurement, and vertical markets such as health care and manufacturing. When reviewing your own objectives, it is useful to examine such solution sets, as they may provide a significant head start toward solving your particular requirements. More important, solutions based on integrated technologies and tools often have faster implementations and can be supported effectively as one offering rather than several products. Use of an integrated solution can also have benefits in reduced training requirements.

The Accelerated Solution

As noted earlier, large vendors have started to deliver targeted solutions around their enterprise server families. One example of this is the Microsoft Solution for Supplier Enablement. Although the core server products in the solution—Commerce Server 2000, BizTalk Server 2000, and SQL Server 2000—already provide much of the functionality required for a supplier to be effective, certain additions are required to deliver a solution truly targeted at addressing suppliers' needs and objectives.

The Microsoft BizTalk Accelerator for Suppliers, also included in the solution, brings these core servers together. The BizTalk Accelerator for Suppliers provides built-in intelligence to provide trading partner management, catalog publishing, order processing, and remote shopping with the leading electronic procurement and e-marketplaces

---

(continued)

The Accelerated Solution *(continued)*

standards and applications. It can also be extended to accommodate additional electronic sales channels. It adds the following supplier-specific functionality to the offering:

- Intelligent adapters are provided for common industry trading standards, such as cXML (Ariba, Clarus, and others) and xCBL/OCI (SAP, Commerce One, and others). These provide the ability to publish product information to customers, including the conversion of the catalog data from the supplier's native format into that of the customer, regardless of the procurement systems they use.

- Remote shopping support (also referred to as round-trip, tap-out, or punch-out) is provided, including prebuilt templates and a complete prebuilt solution site.

- Once you start dealing with multiple channels, the requirements for managing these channels and extracting business intelligence become more complex. For this reason, the BizTalk Accelerator for Suppliers also includes prebuilt user interfaces for managing this information. These include the following:

  - Trading Partner Manager, in which a supplier manages the many relationships with customers and the methods they use to purchase.

  - Catalog Publisher, in which a supplier matches those relationships with the right product information and manages the publishing of that information to customers.

  - Order Manager, in which orders from many customers can be captured, viewed, and managed, in addition to managing them in existing ordering systems.

- The final part of the BizTalk Accelerator for Suppliers consists of detailed guidance and documentation on how to configure systems using the Accelerator and the core enterprise servers. This is not just product documentation but includes concrete information on how to implement effective supplier-centric systems, including guidance and standard configuration options for

> ### The Accelerated Solution   *(continued)*
>
> small, medium, and large suppliers. Other related information is
> also included, such as how to create an intelligent firewall to
> protect and secure such a system and how to use the included
> integration tools to perform supplier-centric integration with
> existing technology investments such as ERP systems and so on.
>
> By providing the features just described, the BizTalk Accelerator for
> Suppliers turns a set of individual products into an integrated solution.

Hardware and Infrastructure

We have now covered the software aspect of your solution. However, do not
forget that there will also be a hardware and infrastructure component. To
deliver a scalable solution, you will need to procure and configure the
machines that will host your e-commerce software. You must provide appropriate Internet connectivity and ensure that there is sufficient network bandwidth (a large enough "pipe" to the Internet) so that your customers will be
able to access your systems when they need to.

Again, you may balk at this level of consideration, especially if you intend
to outsource the hosting of your system to a service provider. However, you
should still quantify the levels of system and network performance you expect
from the overall solution and use this as a benchmark when assessing service
providers.

Reusing Successful Solutions

One of the advantages of bringing in a third-party consultant, whether a system integrator or a vendor, is that they can bring with them a set of proven
solution architectures for the type of system you require. Work is in progress
in various areas to try to identify and publicize common patterns found in
e-commerce systems. These patterns describe a particular solution and why
it is built that way. A pattern describes the issues that need to be addressed
and how the particular solution solves them.

Such patterns can be very useful to your own IT staff when they are looking
to evaluate or create solutions. The patterns will vary from general architectural

patterns through to precise, prescriptive guidance on how and where to apply specific products. All of this is useful in speeding up implementation and avoiding the pitfalls that other people have already encountered.

Preintegrated solutions, as discussed in the sidebar "The Accelerated Solution," encapsulate this type of experience in a complete offering that wraps up the basic products with targeted functionality to help deliver rapid supplier solutions. Such solutions are based on repeatable processes and requirements and are designed to be flexible in the face of a changing environment. Also, by using such an offering, your efforts will be backed by trained implementers and a one-stop support infrastructure.

Creating a Plan

By now you should have absorbed a lot of information about B2B e-commerce and its possibilities for your organization. You will probably want to put some of them into practice. Therefore, the next stage is to build a team and create a plan.

Romancing the Stakeholders

One of the key things to ensure is that you have the right people on your side. Any initiative that has as large an impact on a business as B2B e-commerce must have support from the very top of the company; otherwise it is almost inevitably doomed to failure. Before spending too much time on a potential solution, sound out people at appropriate levels of the company to see if they perceive the benefit of such an initiative as a priority. If they do not, then you will need to spend most of your initial efforts on selling the concept to these people before coming up with a concrete plan.

To gain buy-in at the executive level, you will need to ensure that other key personnel in your company also back your strategy. This will obviously include the IT management team, but it should also include any parts of the organization that will be affected by the new systems, such as sales, marketing, or customer support. If such groups do not get the opportunity to provide input to the plans, they may perceive them as a threat, rather than an opportunity, and possibly hinder progress or even prevent the plans from gaining approval.

Finally, when selling the idea of B2B e-commerce, it is important to set an appropriate level of expectation in terms of time frames, money, and business benefits. Excessive expectations can make a relatively successful project appear as a failure in the eyes of those to whom it has been oversold.

Selecting Partners

Early in your planning, you should identify appropriate partners who can contribute to the plan. These partners could be third-party systems integrators, product vendors or, most important, customers. All of the partners should be included as far as possible in the decision-making processes to ensure that everyone understands what functionality is required and how it should all fit together. Again, this is where customer input is key: there is no point in building a better mousetrap if your customers do not want to catch mice.

Getting the Ball Rolling

Once you have sold the concept at the executive level, you will gather stakeholders and partners to produce a plan. Initially, as with all other proposed business changes, you need to create a business plan that spells out the potential benefits and risks of your B2B initiative. You should try to quantify such benefits and risks as far as possible and try to remain somewhat objective in your assessments. It is easy to get fired up with enthusiasm for new possibilities, but if solutions are built without preparing for the associated risks, some people can end up being just fired should the solution not live up to expectations.

Summary: Implementing a Solution

There are many different aspects to a solution. The key is to correctly assess your requirements and then to work with trusted partners, both inside and outside the organization, to build an appropriate solution to deliver these requirements. In addition to assessing negative risks, you should be prepared for success and the required scalability requirements that would come along with it.

Because the B2B e-commerce initiative will likely form a key part of your business, you must ensure that it is built on a firm foundation of enterprise-class hardware and software solutions. Where possible, exploit the experience of others, whether that is encapsulated in the functionality of such solutions or in the heads of experienced, trained consultants. Remember, although you are a specialist in your business, you will not be the first, or last, organization to implement B2B e-commerce and your requirements may not be as unique as you think.

Managing the Future: Buyers, Suppliers, and Business-to-Business E-Commerce

We introduced this book with a discussion of the notable changes in trading practices that have occurred in the past, from the Agricultural Revolution, through the Industrial Revolution, to the currently emerging Internet-based business environment. We are in the middle of a revolution in which information is one of the key assets that buyers and suppliers use to support their trading practices. The exchange of business information between trading partners, using the Internet, now allows goods and services to be bought and sold with unprecedented speed and efficiency. The reach of suppliers that take advantage of this infrastructure has been extended to include nearly every business in the world as a potential customer, and buyers can now build stronger relationships with these empowered suppliers, wherever they are located. The technology and infrastructure that support these trading opportunities are still maturing, but until extraterrestrial markets appear, these opportunities are about as good as it gets.

Although we have concentrated on the issues and opportunities for suppliers so far in this book, we use a slightly different perspective for this chapter. We examine business-to-business (B2B) e-commerce from the perspective of both suppliers *and* their business customers. In doing so, we will discuss the benefits that these customers can achieve by using empowered suppliers and how suppliers can present their most attractive propositions to those buyers.

We conclude this book by providing advice about how to increase agility and improve your company's ability to manage change as it occurs. This advice includes some pointers on choosing your investments in technology wisely and managing and protecting those investments in the face of rapidly evolving business environments. This applies equally to all participants in the B2B e-commerce arena.

Buyers and Suppliers: Moving into the Information Age

Now is the time for both suppliers and buyers to exploit the Internet in their business strategies. Whether you are responsible for your company's sales and marketing, purchasing, supply chain, or multiple functions, you should look closely at the structure of your current business to maximize the advantages you can gain by using technology (specifically the Internet) as a strategic weapon. Is that structure more suited to trading in the Industrial Age, rather than the Information Age? If so, you may need to re-examine it. Trading with other businesses over the Internet will likely require you to make changes to your business processes, the way in which your employees interact with those processes, and the way in which you build strategic relationships with your trading partners. Such changes should be viewed in a positive light; these changes will allow you thrive in the new business environment, not just survive. You will be able to compete more effectively and take advantage of opportunities that did not exist a few years ago, and you will be able to shape your company so that it is more responsive to market conditions than ever before. You will also remain flexible enough to take advantage of any new business models that may emerge.

The Buyer's Perspective: The Benefits of Partnering with Empowered Suppliers

If you are on the purchasing side of your organization, you will have certain business objectives that you want to achieve as you embrace B2B e-commerce as part of your procurement strategies. If you are a supplier, you would be well advised to understand these objectives from the viewpoint of your business customers. The following list describes the most common objectives, from the perspective of a buyer:

- **Reduction in procurement transaction costs.** Probably *the* most important B2B e-commerce objective, for most purchasing organizations, is the reduction of costs associated with the procurement process. The cost of each transaction is largely tied to the amount of time employees spend processing the data that underpins the purchasing process. Improving the efficiency of the procurement process by reducing the amount of manual processing involved directly reduces these costs. Table 6-1 (p. 158) compares a typical manual procurement process with an automated one. The steps are not restricted to those undertaken by the buyer organization; they also include those taken by suppliers and all participants in the fulfillment process.

- **Increases in efficiency for all employees.** As discussed in *Chapter 1, "The Role of Suppliers in Business-to-Business E-Commerce,"* there is a benefit of streamlining the procurement process that might be even more important for some organizations than a simple reduction in transaction costs. This benefit derives from the increased efficiency that an automated procurement system can deliver for *all* employees at your organization.

- **Improved supplier response times for business transactions.** Buyers aim to achieve efficient integration with their suppliers to enable those companies to fulfill purchase orders in an efficient and timely manner. Not only does an automated procurement system reduce the transaction costs for making purchases, it also allows products and services to be delivered more quickly and on a more consistently predictable basis than was traditionally possible.

- **Minimizing other operational overheads.** In addition to transaction costs, buyers seek to reduce many other operational overheads through their B2B e-commerce strategies. One such example is the aim of reducing surplus inventory by operating within a value chain that is fully integrated with their suppliers.

- **Reducing errors in the procurement process.** As described in Table 6-1, automated procurement systems can reduce (or even eradicate) errors associated with the manual processing of data. Not only does this ensure that you purchase the correct products, at the correct price, from the correct supplier (thereby tightening your value chain operations), but also that your employees will not waste time (and therefore money) constructing purchase orders, only for them to be rejected because of a typographical or similar error.

- **Reducing maverick spending.** By having employees use standard Web-based applications for placing orders, a much higher percentage of a company's spending can be funneled through preferred suppliers. This allows your company to take advantage of predefined discounts and allows your purchases to be tracked and accounted for effectively. *Maverick spending* refers to purchases that are made outside of these standard purchasing methods. For example, even though a company may have a preferred vendor that provides catering for internal meetings, many employees might be tempted to call their favorite restaurant to place their order, eliminating the company's ability to track this spending by supplier and category (because the charges are usually funneled through expense reports instead of the purchasing department) and usually resulting in higher expenses.

Table 6-1. Manual Versus Automated Procurement

Manual Procurement	Automated Procurement
1. Obtain product information. The employee looking to procure goods must obtain product information directly from suppliers, from their own corporate purchasing department, or from other assisting parties such as administrative assistants. Contacting several suppliers might be necessary to receive current prices and descriptions.	**1. Online discovery of product information.** The buyer can search and view product information from consolidated electronic catalogs. These catalogs contain products from many suppliers. The individual suppliers can keep their product information updated by publishing the latest product information that is to be included in the catalog. Some of the product information may be accessed directly from the supplier's integrated site through remote shopping (see *Chapter 3, "Technology as a Strategic Weapon for Suppliers"*).
2. Create an order. The employee, administrative assistant, or purchasing agent must complete a paper-based form. Information such as prices, product details, cost-center codes, and vendor codes must be manually entered, which can result in errors and can take a significant amount of time to gather and complete.	**2. Simplified order creation.** The employee completes a Web-based form. Much of the required information, such as cost codes, prices, product information, and vendor codes can be provided automatically or chosen from drop-down lists and similar interface features. This can reduce or even eradicate errors. Alternatively, fully automated procurement systems might detect low stock levels of products and automatically place orders, without requiring human intervention.
3. Obtain approval. In many cases, the employee must seek approval from a relevant supervisor or manager. The authorization might require signatures from several managers, and it is usually the responsibility of the individual employee to obtain all required approvals.	**3. Intelligent approval process.** The automated procurement application can automatically submit the order to the correct individual for approval using electronic methods such as e-mail or instant messaging applications. Where more than one individual is involved in the approval process, the order can be automatically routed to each individual as approval is obtained.

(continued)

Table 6-1.   Manual Versus Automated Procurement   *(continued)*

4. Submit the order.	**4. Automatic submission of orders.**
After approval has been obtained, manual purchase orders must be generated. Because the order form may include products from more than one supplier, a separate purchase order must be created for each company. These orders must then be mailed or faxed to suppliers.	After approval has been obtained, the order can be processed to separate the products from different suppliers. Purchase orders can then be automatically created for each supplier. Depending on your purchasing strategy, the orders can be placed immediately with the supplier, or multiple orders can be combined on a daily, weekly, or cost basis before purchase orders are sent.
5. Fulfill the order.	**5. Automatic fulfillment of orders.**
The supplier receives the paper-based order and must check whether the product is in stock and whether the pricing information is correct. The supplier can then fulfill the order. If the order is rejected for any reason, the buyer must be contacted and the process repeated.	Supplier systems can process the electronically received order. After the information is automatically validated, supplier systems (such as inventory, billing, and so on) can fulfill the order. If the order is rejected (on the basis of price, out-of-stock products, or for any other reason), the buyer's system can be notified automatically and without significant delays.
6. Ship the goods.	**6. Automatic tracking of the shipping process.**
The supplier ships the goods (or uses a fulfillment company to do so). The buyer has no knowledge of the arrival date for the products unless he or she has contacted the supplier (or shipper) to track the status of the order, or unless there is a service level agreement guaranteeing delivery within a certain time frame.	Automated links between the buying organization's systems and those of the supplier (or other participants in the process) allow the buyer to track the progress of the order online.

(continued)

Table 6-1.   Manual Versus Automated Procurement   *(continued)*

7. Receive the goods.	7. Automated inventory processes.
The goods are delivered to, and processed by, the receiving department at the buying organization. This department must then identify the individual employee and deliver the goods to him or her.	As products arrive at the buying organization, their details are entered into the system that tracks received goods. This system can match the products to the submitted orders and provide details about which individual the goods should be delivered to, tracking the entire process throughout.
8. Pay for the goods.	**8. Automated payment.**
When the arrival of the goods is confirmed, the payment process begins, and can take significant amounts of time and effort on the part of both buyers and suppliers. Often at this stage, there is still no guarantee that the goods have made their way to the individual who ordered them.	The system might require the individual employee to confirm that he or she received the goods and that they function as expected. This confirmation might be used as a trigger to automatically pay the supplier for the goods.

Although we have used the process of ordering simple goods in this comparison, the procurement of complex goods or professional services would bear a similar comparison, but it would have many additional or more complicated processes with even higher risks, adding even further benefits to automated methods.

Although you may have many other objectives specific to your company, the key point that you must understand as a buyer is that you will only maximize the benefits of electronic procurement if you can partner with fully empowered suppliers. Those suppliers will want to run their businesses in a manner that allows them to adjust to your changing needs rapidly, but they will only be able to do so if they, too, can realize significant benefits to their business in the process. Some buyers have attempted to force their suppliers to integrate with a particular system or business model, but we advise against taking this stance, as it has proven to be highly unsuccessful. Most suppliers have shown that they simply will not participate in business models that provide them with poor value. Instead, you need to view your suppliers as essential trading partners, so you can both collaborate for mutual benefit and their success can have a direct impact on your own success.

Suppliers: Matching Your Business Objectives with Those of Your Business Customers

We have discussed the benefits that buyers are looking to achieve from auto-mating their procurement process. Quite simply, you will become a very attractive proposition, as a supplier, if you can understand the buyers' per-spective and help them achieve those benefits.

All of this does not mean that you should relinquish your goal of remain-ing empowered as a supplier. Far from it! Remaining empowered, flexible, and able to respond to market conditions is essential if you are to offer high value to your business customers. Although the bulk of this book has addressed issues from the supplier's perspective, you should certainly devise your strate-gies with your business customers' objectives in mind. Incorporating B2B e-commerce into your selling strategies will allow you to offer this high value and enable you to achieve all of the other objectives we have discussed throughout this book. Just as we advise buyers to view their suppliers as criti-cal business partners, we also advise you to build strong, collaborative, strate-gic relationships with these business customers. That way, you can stay abreast of their changing needs and respond to them in a timely manner.

Managing Change

Keeping up-to-date with new business models is a challenge. Keeping up with the technology that enables these business models is even more chal-lenging, especially since the introduction of the Internet. Attempting to man-age and *synchronize* these changes together might seem daunting. To respond to the changes in business models, you will need to develop a technology infrastructure that can be modified quickly and without great difficulty or expense. Basically, you need an infrastructure that assumes tomorrow will be different from today and has been built with change in mind. This issue faces both suppliers and buyers.

Synchronizing Technology Changes with Business Initiatives

As soon as one set of technology changes have been achieved, allowing you to serve a particular customer requirement or take advantage of a particular business model, you may find that further modifications are then required, as the model will have evolved. These changes might actually be small, but they are vital to your continued success. They need to be implemented quickly and easily if you are to maintain an advantage as you move your company forward. The two major areas that you will constantly need to manage, as well as reassess from time to time, are the business models within which your company operates and the technology that supports those models. Because some of the business models in the new economy are proving to be transient in nature, the technology-based solutions that allow you to participate should have similar flexibility. An application that supports your buying or selling strategy today may be no longer useful in 12 months when you want to take advantage of some new business initiative, not to mention changes that may have occurred within your company. You will, of course, want to replace that particular solution with one that is more suitable.

If you think that all of this is daunting, you are correct. Traditionally, businesses have been unable to afford applications and IT infrastructure that may only have a life span of a few months. Furthermore, large IT systems and solutions have traditionally taken months, if not years, to be designed, developed, tested, and then rolled out. Obviously, spending large amounts of money on a solution every few months is not a viable option, and taking significant time to develop any one of these solutions simply will not work. The problems that you will face in the new business environment, then, are twofold. The first problem lies in simply keeping abreast of changes in rapidly evolving business models. The second is ensuring that your IT solutions evolve apace with your business strategies. You must achieve all of this without requiring huge investments for every change and without having to dispose of existing (and expensive) IT infrastructure.

Creating Dynamic Solutions

Given that we cannot predict the changes to business models that may occur, even in six months, keeping your company up-to-date with new opportunities is something that only you and the other stakeholders at your company can do. What *we* can do, however, is offer advice on how to choose solutions that are built for change and how to keep those solutions abreast of changes in a timely and affordable manner. The most important issue that you will need to address is that any solution you commission as you embrace B2B e-commerce must be able to evolve along with your business; that is, it must be flexible and extensible. The way to achieve this is to build a solid core for your IT infrastructure, supplemented with dynamic applications that operate on its periphery. (We will discuss these applications later.)

The Core

The core should address all of the technology needs for running your business on a day-to-day basis. For example, the core will contain your human resources system, your inventory database, your enterprise resource planning (ERP) and accounting applications (such as accounts payable, accounts receivable, and so on), and any other system that your company uses internally to function. Although the functionality in the core may need occasional modifications or updating, these systems are certainly not as volatile as the technology needed to interface with the new Internet-based business models. In fact, you have most likely been using these systems in the non–B2B e-commerce world. Such systems often involve considerable development effort and cost, but they typically remain useful for many years. It is likely that you already have some (or many) of these core systems, so you will just have to think about how they can operate (and cooperate) with the more transient solutions that allow you to rapidly adjust your business models.

The Periphery

As discussed already, you will need to develop solutions rapidly at comparatively low cost if you are to take advantage of the changing nature of B2B e-commerce. Although we place these applications on the periphery of your solid IT core, we are not implying that they are peripheral to your business. Far from it: these applications form the business solutions that deliver your e-commerce strategies. Rather, the term *periphery* indicates that these systems provide a gateway for the exchange of data and services between your trading partners and your core systems. The software that provides a bridge between your core systems and these new channels takes the form of *dynamic* applications. These applications can be developed quickly and inexpensively and changed with relatively minimal effort. If you have a solid core, and some standard ways of interfacing with that core, then developing such dynamic applications is possible, even within the budgetary and time constraints imposed in the B2B e-commerce arena. This is because these new applications are largely focused on exposing and repackaging the functionality of the core systems for each new audience. If the core business systems are designed well, and there is a consistent framework on which to build the applications, then they can be rapidly assembled.

The Core-Periphery Interface

It is critical to the success of building the applications on the periphery that they can communicate with your core systems in standard ways. If you have to redefine how an application exchanges data with each of your core systems every time a new B2B solution is required, you will not be able to implement these new applications within an appropriate time frame or a reasonable budget. Rather than requiring software developers to revisit this issue for every new application, you can instead implement standard interfaces that allow the exchange of business data between your core systems and your B2B applications.

Figure 6-1 illustrates the whole model. The internal systems do not provide a consistent means of communication, but these differences are smoothed away by the core-periphery interfaces.

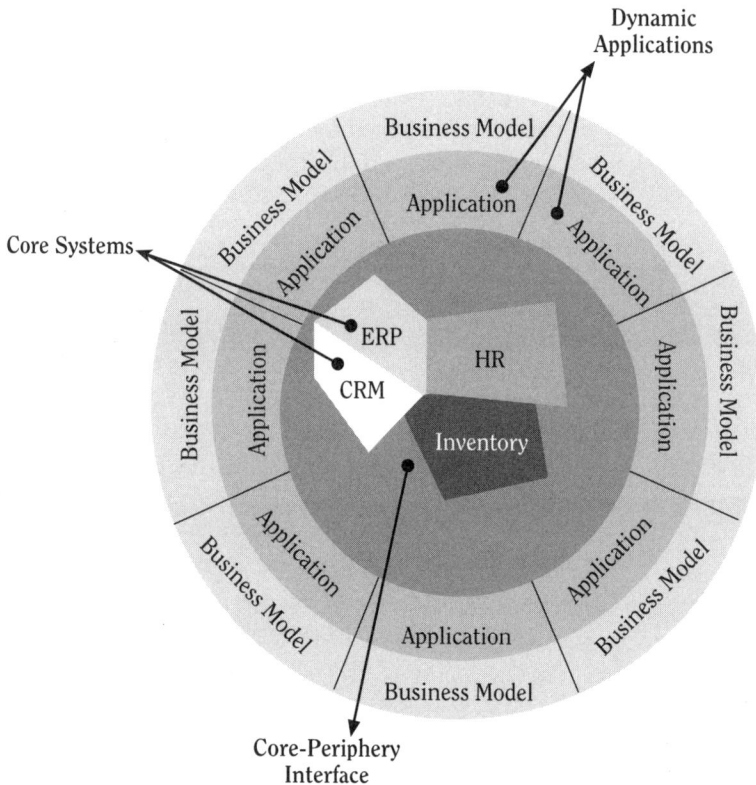

Figure 6-1.   *Designing dynamic solutions. As one business model is replaced with another, you can quickly and easily adapt applications that exchange data with your core systems in a standardized manner. The interface between these dynamic applications and the core is critical in allowing quick and cost-effective development.*

Protecting Your Investments

For your IT infrastructure to adapt to business models that are constantly evolving, you will need to ensure that it exhibits two primary characteristics: extensibility and scalability.

Ensuring Extensibility

In practice, protecting your existing and new core IT investments and ensuring extensibility involves using industry standards as you expose this infrastructure and add new functionality. In a nutshell, this means implementing and using many of the following core Internet standards:

- **Hypertext Transfer Protocol (HTTP) for transport.** HTTP is the most widely used transport protocol on the Internet. HTTP standards are governed by the World Wide Web Consortium (W3C). All modern Internet-enabled applications communicate using HTTP, so you will certainly not want to buck this trend.

- **Extensible Markup Language (XML) for data description.** XML standards are also governed by the W3C and are not tied to any particular software vendor's products. In recent years, there has been almost complete industry acceptance of XML as *the* data description language for B2B e-commerce, as well as for many other types of applications.

- **Universal Description, Discovery, and Integration (UDDI) for describing services and functionality.** UDDI enables online, automatic discovery of service information and allows you to build flexible, yet manageable, systems. UDDI is fast becoming an accepted standard for allowing applications and services to interoperate.

Some of your core systems may be capable of using XML-based communication mechanisms already, in which case you should definitely take advantage of that on the inner surface of the core-periphery applications. For any core systems that are not capable of using XML directly, the interface itself should translate data between XML and non-XML formats. Integration servers, such as those described in *Chapter 5, "Implementing a Solution,"* can provide the foundations needed for these translations. Many prebuilt adapters are available for use by integration servers, but they are most often just a starting point because all implementations are unique, making the tools for building and adapting these components critical. The time and money spent building (or buying) these interfaces are necessary investments, but ones that will pay for themselves many times over as you realize the ability to quickly and inexpensively adapt to changing environments.

The outer surface of the core-periphery interface should be completely XML-enabled. Having an extensible, flexible interface, into which you can simply plug applications, is the reason for having the interface in the first place. If there is no standard way of communicating on this surface of the interface, then it serves no point. You may as well write applications that communicate directly with the core systems.

Ensuring Scalability

As your company grows, you may need to increase the horsepower of your solutions to process increased throughput or meet increased business functionality requirements. You might add more computers, faster processors, more memory, larger disks, and so on to your existing machines, or you might replace outdated machines with bigger and faster ones. Whatever your approach, you will want to make sure that your infrastructure can adjust to changing demand in a cost-effective manner. The term *scalability* is most often used in the IT profession to describe the relationship between increases in computing power and the ability to service more demand. There are many technical issues that affect scalability that we do not even go into here, but the important point is that a system is said to be scalable if an increase in computing power produces a comparable increase in the demand that can be serviced (or the rate at which a constant demand can be satisfied).

You may find it useful to consider scalability in terms of resource *cost* against *performance*. Figure 6-2 compares this relationship for scalable and nonscalable solutions.

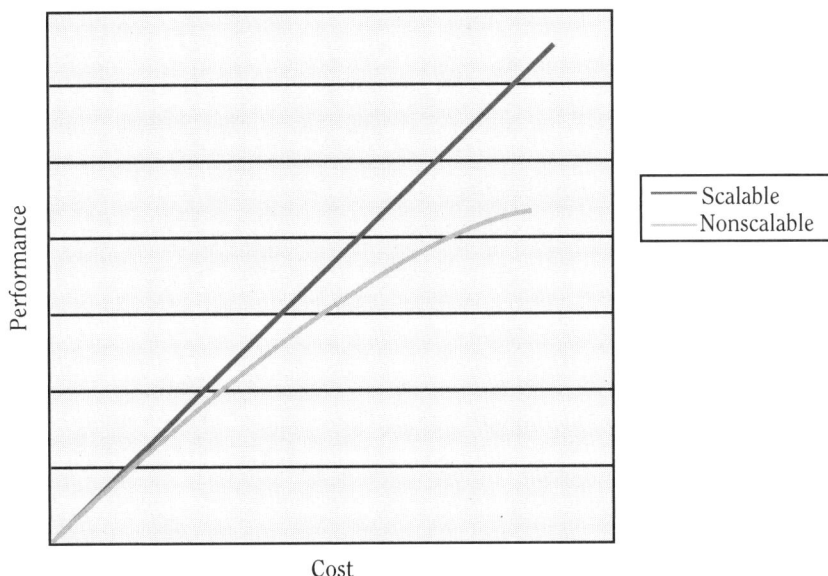

Figure 6-2.   *Scalable versus nonscalable solutions. The scalable solution maintains a certain ratio between cost and performance. The nonscalable solution is characterized by diminishing returns of performance on cost, as higher levels of performance are required.*

You must be concerned with the scalability of all parts of your IT infrastructure. The way to ensure that a lack of scalability does not become an issue is to use solutions based on enterprise-class server products, such as the database servers, commerce servers, and integration servers we discussed in *Chapter 5, "Implementing a Solution."*

Summary: Managing the Future

The idea of using the Internet to trade goods and services will be with us for a long time to come. We are currently still in the infancy of the Information Revolution as it affects commercial organizations and trade. Many new opportunities will appear in the near future, and you will want to evaluate and take advantage of these prospects intelligently. New markets will appear and disappear at an unprecedented rate. Some business models will survive for only a short time, and you may want to participate in some of these while they are there. Others will gain a stronger foothold and set the standards for how business is conducted in the future. You will definitely want to make sure that you can participate in many of *these* business opportunities. In short, you will want to take advantage of high-value propositions and avoid poor ones as B2B e-commerce evolves.

The technology that will provide your company with the required agility for surviving and prospering in this volatile environment now exists, but that technology necessitates careful planning and management. Used wisely, technology can become a strategic weapon that you can use in your business strategies, rather than just an additional cost of doing business.

We will allow ourselves one prediction to conclude this book. Once you have taken the initial step of embracing B2B e-commerce, the subsequent changes in the way you buy and sell goods and services will best be described in terms of evolution rather than revolution.

Empowering Kunkle Valve: A Business Value Case Study

In less than 4 months Kunkle Valve, a company within Tyco International Ltd., implemented a Microsoft-based supplier enablement solution resulting in expanded overall sales, increased customer satisfaction, and reduced operational costs.

Note Kunkle Valve, a leading manufacturer of quality safety and relief valve products for industrial and commercial applications is a company within the Flow Control division of Tyco International Ltd., a $28.9 billion global manufacturer with 300,000 employees that has leadership positions in flow control products, electrical and electronic components, and underwater telecommunications systems.

A business value analysis, using the Rapid Economic Justification (REJ) framework audited by Gartner Measurement, validated that the supplier enablement solution from Microsoft will enable the Kunkle Valve Division to extend its market reach and gain new international sales, accounting for a minimum expected overall sales growth of 5 percent. From implementing this e-commerce solution, Kunkle expects to expand internationally and reduce annual operating costs. Reducing order entry errors by 60 percent helped reduce order processing costs by 50 percent. These improvements enhanced customer satisfaction by reducing product returns by 50 percent and reducing time to receive orders directly into Kunkle Valve's manufacturing system by 65 percent. Tyco achieved this value by deploying the supplier enablement solution for less than $400,000. The e-commerce Web site went from concept to "live" in less than 4 months using minimal IT resources, enabling Kunkle to achieve a 94 percent internal rate of return (IRR) and begin realizing a return on investment only 3 months after deployment.

Note   The REJ showed a 94 percent IRR based on increased sales from international market reach, improving operating margin, and increasing customer and supplier satisfaction.

Technology Enablers

- **Agility.** Rapid deployment enables quick market expansion. Catalog integration via XML results in easier supply-chain efficiencies.

- **Scalability.** Easy-to-update online catalog; creates customer-specific promotions or pricing.

- **Availability.** Allows any Web-enabled company to be a customer or a supplier. Low cost of entry.

- **Supportability.** Easy for non-IT business person to implement and maintain. Low cost of ownership.

Executive Summary

Kunkle Valve, a leading manufacturer of quality safety and relief valve products for industrial and commercial applications, and a division of Tyco Valves and Controls, of Tyco International Ltd., developed a business-to-business (B2B) Web site and back-end infrastructure that enabled it to effectively conduct global e-commerce while improving operational efficiencies throughout its order entry and assembly process. Making use of key components of the Microsoft Solution for Supplier Enablement based on Microsoft's .NET Enterprise Servers product line, Kunkle Valve implemented a business solution that was extremely cost-effective, quick to deploy, and non–resource-intensive for the company's IT department. Using the core supplier enablement solution products—Microsoft Commerce Server, Microsoft BizTalk Server, and Microsoft SQL Server operating on Microsoft Windows 2000 Advanced Server—Kunkle Valve has made it possible for its customers to easily and simply transact business over the Internet. For example, customers can now make purchases and check order and payment status, shipping information, pricing, and product configuration via a direct connection to Kunkle Valve's back-office enterprise resource planning (ERP), inventory, and manufacturing systems. This has decreased the company's order entry errors by 60 percent and decreased its order processing costs by 50 percent, resulting in a higher operating margin and improved customer satisfaction by reducing customer call time for receiving orders by 65 percent. Table A-1 shows the critical success factors, technology enablers, and business benefits for the Microsoft Solution for Supplier Enablement implementation at Kunkle Valve.

Note   The Microsoft Solution for Supplier Enablement is composed of .NET Enterprise Server products combined with the Microsoft BizTalk Accelerator for Suppliers and specialized support. At the time Kunkle Valve implemented its e-business Web site, the complete Solution for Supplier Enablement program was not yet in effect. Therefore, this case study references the supplier enablement solution in the context of specific Microsoft products used by Kunkle Valve, a division of Tyco Valves and Controls of Tyco International Ltd.

Table A-1.   Critical Success Factors, Technology Enablers, and Business Benefits

Critical Success Factor	Technology Enabler	Business Benefits
Increase sales	Agility: creating new platform for growth	Overall sales ↑ > 5 percent International sales ↑ 100 percent Operating margin improved Time that sales has for direct customer interaction ↑ 35 percent
Reduce costs of operations	Supportability: automated operations and business processes	Order entry errors ↓ 60 percent Order time to manufacturing ↓ 65 percent Order processing costs ↓ 50 percent Order processing full-time equivalent (FTEs) ↓ 20 percent
Improve customer satisfaction	Availability: easier way of doing business with customers and suppliers at lower cost	Customer call time per sale ↓ 65 percent Customer procurement related costs ↓ Customer product returns ↓ 50 percent Customer service requests ↓ Customer fulfillment cycle time ↓
Improved decision making	Manageability: real-time analytics	Integrated logistics ↑ 100 percent Automated financials < 30 minutes to run company-wide reports

"The Solution for Supplier Enablement by Microsoft enabled us to take a quantum leap in serving our global Flow Control business customers while improving operational efficiencies," said L. Dennis Kozlowski, Chief Executive Officer and Chairman of the Board of Tyco International Ltd. "We have opened up new international markets at very little cost and have reduced our cost of sales, and in turn freed up cash flow. We anticipate saving approximately 1 percent—about $300 million—of our total revenue in direct operational expenses over the next 3 years by implementing these solutions across multiple business units."

The Solution for Supplier Enablement was implemented into Kunkle Valve's existing IT environment in less than 4 months by 2 business managers using minimal IT resources. An REJ analysis audited by Gartner Measurement, a business unit of the GartnerGroup, identified that the company achieved a 94 percent IRR. Kunkle Valve received an initial return on investment (ROI) only 3 months after implementation. As a result of a successful deployment at Kunkle Valve, Tyco International Ltd. is looking at implementing similar supplier enablement solutions in many of its other business units.

Improved Operational Efficiency: Automated Order Entry Process Streamlines Operations and Improves Operating Margin

As with many industrial manufacturing companies, the existing manual paper-based business processes at Kunkle Valve required a high level of human interaction and redundancy that was prone to multiple errors. Two business managers at the company knew that if they could automate and Web-enable the company's order entry process, they would also see efficiencies throughout their value chain. To this end, these managers initiated a pilot project to streamline the order entry process using Microsoft's supplier enablement solution. Their intention was to reduce order entry errors and the time required for processing—compared with the existing fax-based manual order entry process—and improve overall operations.

As the project matured, executive management recognized the overarching potential of influencing business processes throughout the company. As a result, four critical success factors for business value were identified:

- **Revenue.** Increase sales and expand into international markets.

- **Operational efficiencies.** Reduce internal costs through automating internal processes and by extending supply-chain–specific information to customers, vendors, and partners.

- **Customer satisfaction.** Enhance customer satisfaction with custom 24/7 self-service while reducing the customer's cost of procurement and time for delivery.

- **Executive decision making.** Enhance business agility using real-time analytics.

Figure A-1 depicts the prior fax-based and hand-entry method used by Kunkle Valve for receiving and fulfilling orders from customers based on a manual configuration process.

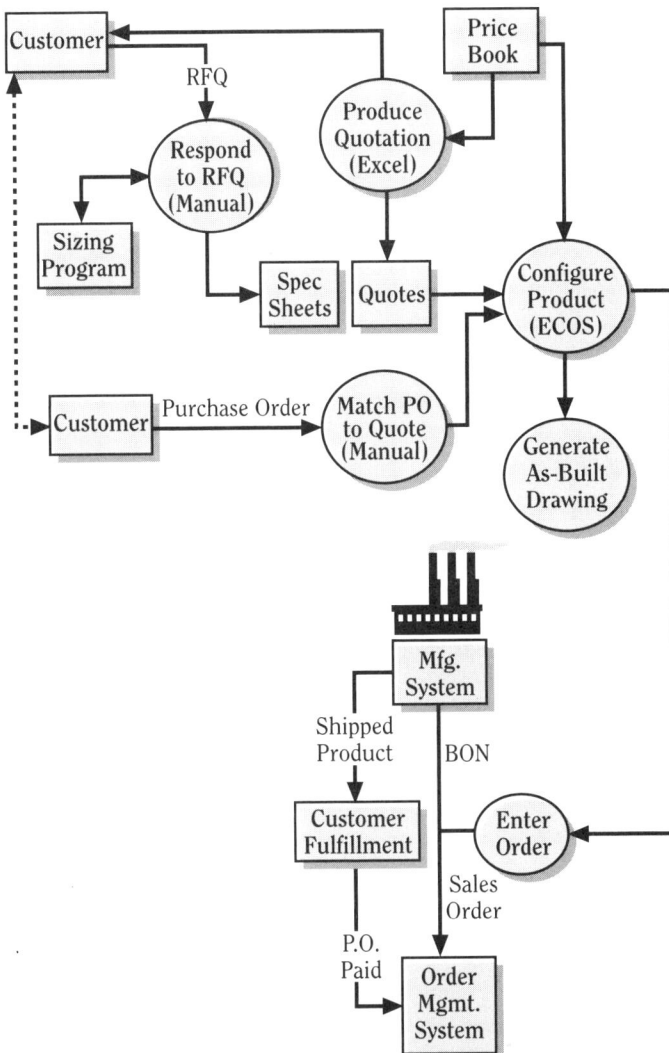

Figure A-1.   *Prior manual and fax-based order entry system.*

Utilizing the supplier enablement solution from Microsoft, Kunkle Valve was able to replace paper-based processes with digital automation for a fast, accurate, customer-centric ordering experience that lowered overhead costs, reduced time of payment cycles, and made it easier for domestic and international customers to do business with them through the Internet. As a result of sales automation efficiencies, sales representatives can now spend 35 percent more time on higher value activities with their customers.

"Making it easy for our customers to purchase from us, with easy payment terms and real-time delivery tracking, is critical for us to reduce lead time, drive down cost of goods, and increase sales," stated Juan Gomez, Vice President Operations Valve Products/Tyco Valves and Controls – North America. "Using the supplier enablement solution [by Microsoft] we were effective in decreasing our administrative overhead while also decreasing order processing errors by 60 percent. This has improved operating margin and increased customer satisfaction. Real-time reporting allows us to share order data with customers and suppliers, identify buying patterns, and offer strategic recommendations to customer purchases. This has enabled our sales reps to spend more time providing higher value services to our customers." Figure A-2 shows the new Web-enabled system that provided customized configuration and ordering, real-time order tracking for customers, and integrated real-time business analytics for Kunkle Valve.

The following sections provide insight into the core operational processes that were modified at Kunkle Valve using the Solution for Supplier Enablement by Microsoft:

1. Order processing.

2. Credit verification and payment processing.

3. Order fulfillment.

4. Real-time operational performance updates enabled by enterprise application integration (EAI).

Kunkle Valve realized an overall revenue increase after automating these core operational processes. Financial benefits were also realized by customers and suppliers throughout the value chain.

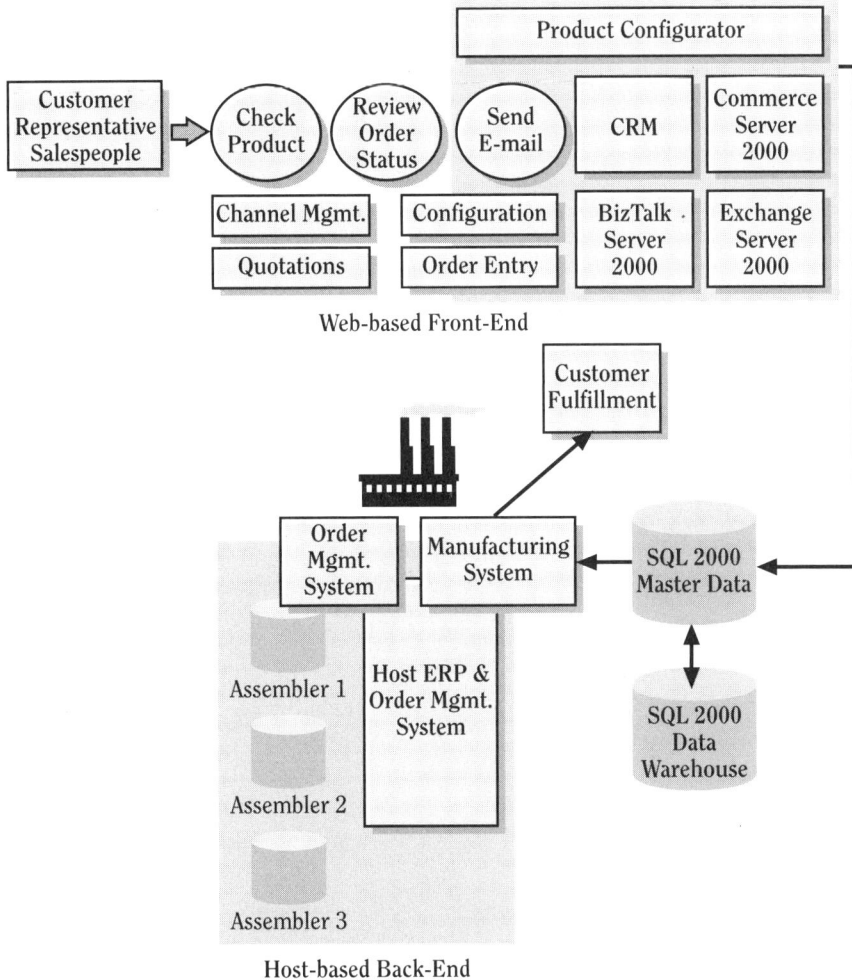

Figure A-2. *Supplier enablement automated configuration and order processing system.*

Improve Operational Efficiency: Automated Ordering Process Reduces Order Entry Errors by 60 Percent

As do many industrial manufacturing companies, Kunkle Valve uses contract assemblers who purchase separate parts from Kunkle Valve and then assemble them based on orders they receive from customers via Kunkle Valve's fax-based inbound ordering and manual rekeying process. However, using fax and manual ordering for over 5000 orders per month, the company experienced incorrect order fulfillment due to handwriting recognition problems, incorrect pricing, and inconsistent follow-up.

Inaccurate orders had a ripple effect throughout the entire company including its product assemblers. Kunkle Valve was often left with fully assembled but essentially nonsaleable custom products after discovering that the finished product delivered to the customer was made to incorrect specifications. With product unit sales prices ranging from $30 to $50 and an average order of $500, already thin margins turned into costs because the assemblers had to be paid based on the order that they received from Kunkle Valve. Not only was there a time delay in shipping the customer a finished product and decrease in customer satisfaction, the assemblers and suppliers were growing increasingly unhappy with having to do double work to complete the same order.

Kunkle Valve found that by automating its existing manual sales order process using the supplier enablement solution, there was a 60 percent reduction in the number of order entry errors. As a result, contract assemblers were happier to get product specifications directly from the customer via a Web-enabled catalog, and subsequently could correctly fulfill orders.

"We needed to automate our fax-based and hand process to minimize errors since these errors increased internal costs and, more importantly, created a huge inconvenience to our customers and suppliers," noted Ellen Roberts, Corporate Controller for Tyco Valves and Controls. "We looked at all aspects of our manual order-entry process and found that each order error cost the company nearly $300." When there is an error, the company incurs the following costs: shipping both ways; overhead time for a number of departments including accounting, finance, sales, manufacturing, and inventory; and rush costs on expediting the correct order to the customer. Roberts continued, "Reducing order errors by automating our entire order entry process was cost-effective for the company, and also provided our customers with the right product in a timely manner. This has enabled us to decrease costs and increase our EBIT [earnings before interest and taxes]."

The business value of reducing the number of order entry errors was calculated as follows: the number of transactions × the percentage of errors × the cost of an error (allocating 15 minutes of time for 5 different operational disciplines plus shipping) to find the historical cost of errors. The result of this was multiplied by the percentage reduction in errors to show a total dollar savings (# transactions × percent of errors × the cost of an error = total cost of errors).

Processing costs per order used to be $75. With the supplier enablement solution, overall internal order processing costs were reduced by 50 percent and product returns were reduced. The amount of money saved by automating this one process nearly covered the cost of implementing the complete solution.

Improve Operational Efficiency: Automating Credit Verification and Payment Processes Reduces Invoicing Costs

Compounding the challenge of erroneous order processing that resulted in incorrect products for the customer were complexities in credit verification, invoicing, and accounts receivable.

Customer payment, especially in situations where an order was delayed due to credit verification that required management approval, cost the company an average of $300 in administrative costs per delayed order as well as the cost of incremental sales. Kunkle Valve decided that if they offered online payment via credit cards the credit verification and payment process would be eased for their customers and, therefore, would not necessitate involving Kunkle Valve management and ancillary costs.

"Using electronic technology to streamline the credit verification and billing process has made it easier and more cost-effective for the company as well as our customers," continued Roberts. "Improving our credit verification process has enabled us to spend more time providing customer service and ensure that our products meet the specifications required by our customers."

By implementing credit card payment, the functional parts of the credit verification and payment process have effectively been outsourced at minimal incremental cost.

Improve Customer Satisfaction: Cost per Order Reduced by 50 Percent Yields More Satisfied Customers

Further compounding order processing and accounts receivable challenges was the integration of the company's ERP and accounting systems and those used by the company's customers and suppliers for invoicing and reconciliation of accounts receivable. Most customers and suppliers did not have accounting or ERP systems that integrated with the company's back-end accounting or inventory infrastructure. Deploying Microsoft's supplier enablement solution, and using eXtensible Markup Language (XML), native to BizTalk Server, Kunkle Valve was able to fully integrate with existing customer and supplier e-procurement and ERP systems and effectively create a seamless custom configuration and ordering process.

Additionally, utilizing the SalesLogix Configuration Engine, the company was quickly able to add advanced product configuration capabilities to Commerce Server 2000 without significant development time, thereby enabling any customer to simply configure complex products and easily place orders online. The SalesLogix Configuration Engine combined with Commerce Server contributed to successfully implementing the supplier enablement solution. Key features of Commerce Server that contributed to improving customer satisfaction include:

- **Business desk catalog publishing and ordering.** Out-of-the-box solution to electronically manage a product catalog and orders through a Web-based interface. No manual or paper processes are required.

- **Easily create customer-specific price lists.** Pricing appropriate to the customer, the customer's geographic area, and the market.

- **Remote shopping.** Enables development of a custom experience for trading partners to jump directly to a Web site, place an order, and have the order automatically created in their procurement application or online shopping basket.

> **Note** SalesLogix (*www.saleslogix.com*) is a partner of Microsoft, offering customer relationship management applications, including the SalesLogix Configuration Engine for customized order configuration.

As a result, Kunkle Valve was able to decrease order processing costs by 50 percent per order and reduce the time it took for the customer to enter an order into Kunkle Valve's manufacturing system. The company was also able to reduce internal order processing personnel by 20 percent of its FTEs and reassign them to other value-added activities.

"We needed to increase our availability and reduce lead-time for sales and delivery. And, we needed to make it easy for our suppliers and assemblers to work with us," noted Bob Whyte, General Manager for Manufacturing at Kunkle Valve Division. "Using the Web for customer self-service orders and invoicing has enabled us to focus on increasing the growth of our market share and improving shareholder value by maximizing sales and increasing operating margin. We've achieved tremendous process efficiencies which has boosted morale at Kunkle Valve and improved relations with our customers and suppliers by making sure that the product ordered is the same product that is produced and delivered. Together, we've created a single integrated and highly effective supply chain."

"Using the telephone and fax-based ordering system took a lot of time and often resulted in not getting the product we specified," explained Maynard Hovland, General Manager of Lam Valves, Inc. "Not only did this cause delays with possible repercussions, it also cost us money. Now that we can order online 24/7 and configure the product exactly to our specification, we are assured of getting what we ordered in the time frame that we need it. Our order fulfillment time has decreased, and equally as important we can track the order throughout the entire configuration, manufacturing, and delivery process. Real-time tracking enables us to improve our own processes and reduce costs."

Improve Decision Making: Enterprise Application Integration Provides Real-Time Overview of Operational Processes and Improves Business Agility

Most companies have discrete silos of information spread throughout their various operating groups. Sales and marketing have customer contacts and order history, finance has accounts receivable and payable, shipping has fulfillment, and management has reports that should integrate information from all business units.

Using the real-time reporting functions of the Microsoft Solution for Supplier Enablement enabled by EAI between BizTalk Server and SQL Server 2000, all information associated with the order processing, inventory assessment, product configuration, payment, and the shipping and delivery process is available to the customer and to the company as it happens in real time. Key features that enabled Kunkle Valve to achieve its business goals are:

- **Real-time business analytics.** Real-time reporting allows for quick insight to market trends and enables appropriate business response for increased sales. Facilitates more effective use of human and financial resources.

- **Integration with back-end accounting systems.** Real-time financial data enhances business decision-making process for increased agility in responding to market needs.

- **Catalog publishing via XML.** Seamless data sharing with customers, suppliers, partners, and e-marketplaces, enabled by BizTalk Server regardless of ERP system.

Real-time online information empowers customers with direct order tracking and provides up-to-the-minute reports for Kunkle Valve managers so that they can make timely decisions based on current data. Information silos are effectively reduced to zero and management can now reprioritize resource allocation based on current and accurate information. Having a real-time snapshot enables more effective strategic planning and decision making. Future capability and flexibility for computing outside the workplace can be enabled, which provides telephony application programming interface (TAPI) and wireless application protocol (WAP) services on mobile phones and personal digital assistants (PDAs) so that mobility can be easily provided to customers, partners, and field staff.

"The supplier enablement solution using Commerce and BizTalk Servers was easy to design, quick to implement, and trouble-free to maintain," noted Jeff Lynch, System Architect and Development Manager at Tyco Valves and Controls, responsible for the design, development, and implementation of the Solution for Supplier Enablement. "The real-time analytics help us identify operational areas where we could improve processes, and they easily and seamlessly integrate with the back-end operations of our customers and suppliers, giving them a moment-by-moment snapshot of the entire order-build-fulfillment process."

Increase Revenue: Online Order Configuration Enables International Expansion and Yields Minimum 5 Percent Increase in Overall Sales

As a global leader in the manufacture of safety and relief valve products, Kunkle Valve has products in use throughout the world as both original equipment and as replacement parts. Though over 95 percent of its existing customers are based in North America, Kunkle Valve was experiencing an increasing number of business opportunities in Europe and especially Latin America. As with many industrial manufacturers that operate on thin margins from products with sales prices that average $30 to $50 U.S., it was not cost-effective to open up international sales offices solely to service these potential new accounts.

Kunkle Valve is implementing a language-specific e-commerce site anticipated to take 50 percent of the time and cost compared to a non-Microsoft supplier-enabled Web site. As a result of such rapid time-to-market, Kunkle Valve anticipates successfully penetrating the Latin American market and increasing overall company sales 5 percent in its first 10 months of operation.

Developing language-specific online catalogs will further enable Kunkle Valve to respectfully respond to local markets and in so doing quickly garner a leading market position.

"Using the supplier enablement solution we are now reaching Latin American markets without the trouble, expense, and time delay of setting up separate sales offices," noted Mark Jordan, Director of Marketing and Sales for Kunkle Valve Division. "We are confident that we can increase our overall revenue by 5 percent and cut our cost-of-sales so that the cost of servicing international markets becomes attractive. Plus, we will no longer have to worry about incorrect orders due to language challenges as the Commerce Server–based online ordering system is simple to understand and easy to use and enables our customers to order in their native language."

Tyco's Rapid Implementation Methodology: Implementation in Under 4 Months and Low Cost of Entry Yields Initial Return on Investment in Less Than 3 Months

Kunkle Valve recognized the opportunity for reducing costs through improved operational efficiency and improving satisfaction of domestic customers, as well as obtaining international sales by utilizing Web-enabled e-commerce. In less than 4 months, the company was able to create an online catalog and, by automating its order entry operations, reduce internal costs for order processing by 50 percent. With an e-commerce–enabled Web site, the company was able to expand internationally and expects to increase overall company sales by 5 percent, all for less than $400,000 of invested capital.

Investigating various e-commerce platforms and B2B portals helped Kunkle Valve clarify its needs and identify several requirements for developing its supplier-enabled e-commerce Web site. Key attributes included:

- **Low cost of entry.** Easy and quick to develop, and simple to upgrade and maintain by people not knowledgeable in IT, utilizing standard hardware and software.

- **Adaptability.** Allows for the creation of new business processes that streamline operations and enhance collaboration and create opportunity across the supply chain.

- **Flexibility.** Multilanguage and multicurrency capable of reaching global markets.

- **Interoperability.** Easily and seamlessly integrates with existing internal IT systems, and with customers, suppliers, and partners who have different IT environments.

After investigating the various e-commerce options, Kunkle Valve turned to the Microsoft Solution for Supplier Enablement for its easy-to-design and implement system and software operating on hardware from Dell Computer Corporation. The company used a Dell BigIP Load Balanced server to manage site activities while using the Dell 2450 server to run Commerce Server 2000, and the Dell 6450 server to run SQL Server 2000 and BizTalk Server 2000 Enterprise Edition. "As a leader in customer-facing e-business, Dell's best practices helped us quickly design a user-friendly front-end," noted Jeff Lynch, System Architect and Development Manager. "Dell's preloaded supplier configurations helped us achieve rapid implementation, enabling us to conduct a quick prototype."

"Utilizing an industry standard approach of Plan-Design-Implement-Manage and Support, we were able to implement baseline functionality and achieve an initial return on investment within 3 months after implementation," continued Lynch. Kunkle Valve took into account the specific needs of, its customers and partners and implemented an open operational environment that provided business value to all participants. Microsoft Consulting Services and Dell provided guidance throughout the project. Lynch continued, "Microsoft and Dell's experience in Web-enabling numerous supplier environments helped us prioritize and focus on automating processes that would drive the greatest return on investment and customer satisfaction. Most importantly, they spent time with our operational decision makers and IT staff to discuss our business needs. They offered great ideas and provided guidance on how best to streamline our operations to the benefit of our customers and our bottom line. The supplier enablement implementation is already showing value in utilizing IT to achieve Tyco's business goals."

Figure A-3 depicts the four stages and business goals that the company achieved.

Project Vision
✓ Conduct transactions via Internet
✓ Improve customer information
✓ Reduce company business costs
✓ Reduce customer business costs

Customer-Driven Design Goals
✓ Account and user management
✓ Product catalog and configuration
✓ Custom pricing/Self-service quotations
✓ Order processing and status
✓ Up selling/cross-selling
✓ Account financial status

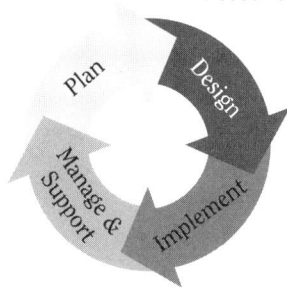

Planned Functional Areas
✓ Login and custom home page
✓ Account/order status
✓ Product selection/configuration
✓ Quotation/order entry
✓ Customer help

Business Objectives
✓ Reduce order entry lead-time
✓ Reduce customer service "phone tag"
✓ Improve customer retention rate
✓ Increase proactive selling time

Figure A-3.   *Plan-Design-Implement-Manage and Support model.*

"The supplier enablement solution offers predictable integration require-ments, which in our implementation came to a little over half of the $400,000 that we spent to deploy the solution," noted Doug Snyder, Director of E-Com-merce for Tyco Valves and Controls. "This included the complete planning and integration into our back-end systems such as ERP. The beauty of investing in a Microsoft technology-based supplier enablement infrastructure is that it forms a highly scalable foundation upon which other Web services and pro-cess automation capabilities can be implemented." Kunkle Valve envisions value being sustained over a number of years by its investment in the .NET Enterprise Servers that provide the foundation for its supplier enablement solution. Snyder continues, "We anticipate obtaining new business value at incremental cost for each new initiative, so the resulting return on invest-ment will be greater for each new project we implement, both at Kunkle Valve and through the various other business units of Tyco [International]."

Even with only baseline functionality, Kunkle Valve has seen cost reduc-tions for the company and its customers. Kunkle Valve expects most of its cus-tomers and vendors to fully adopt and use the system by the end of 2001, achieving some operational and cost efficiency in their respective organizations. The direct benefit of using standard hardware, an essentially "out-of-the-box" solution from Microsoft, and a straightforward design and implementation process enabled the company to build a supplier-enabled Web site with minimal requirements from in-house IT resources.

Supplier Enablement Drives Business Value for Entire Supply Chain

Tyco International Ltd. used the supplier enablement solution at Kunkle Valve as a pilot project to assess the business value of Web-enabling the numerous operating units of the $30 billion global enterprise. Using the REJ framework to assess the business value of the e-commerce solution provided the necessary financial metrics that clearly demonstrated that the supplier enablement solution had met the company's critical success factors of increased growth, improved operational efficiency, and better, more cost-effective ways to interact with customers and suppliers.

"We used our own business requirements and processes and adapted the supplier enablement solution around our needs, rather than being forced into a rigid technological platform that we couldn't control," confirmed Jeff Lynch. "The tools were easy to work with and resulted in an effective design that was quick to implement. We now have seamless connectivity via open standards and protocols that let us easily and conveniently share data with our customers and suppliers. This has enabled us to remain open and available for sales orders 24/7 and has increased our ability to serve our growing international customer base. It has also helped our suppliers gain operational efficiencies that contribute to improving their bottom line."

For More Information

To find more information about Microsoft products and services over the World Wide Web, go to:

- *http://www.microsoft.com/solutions/msse*
- *http://www.microsoft.com/servers*
- *http://www.microsoft.com/net*
- *http://www.microsoft.com/value*
- *http://www.kunklevalve.com*
- *http://www.tyco.com*
- *http://www.gartner.com*
- *http://www.dell.com/supplier*
- *http://www.saleslogix.com*

Microsoft Solution for Supplier Enablement

Microsoft Solution for Supplier Enablement is built on the Microsoft .NET Enterprise Servers, a comprehensive family of server applications designed to deliver rapid time-to-market combined with mission-critical performance, reliability, scalability, and manageability needed by today's global, Web-enabled enterprise. Built for interoperability from the ground up, .NET Enterprise Servers use open Web standards such as XML to enable integrated solutions that move beyond today's world of stand-alone Web sites. Designed to accelerate the development of solutions built on the .NET Enterprise Servers, the Microsoft Solution for Supplier Enablement provides a new set of tools that simplify supplier connectivity to multiple online selling channels.

For more information on Microsoft's e-Business offerings, please visit *http://www.microsoft.com/solutions/msse*.

About This Study

Gartner Measurement, a business unit of The GartnerGroup, has assessed the Tyco International Ltd. and Kunkle Valve REJ study for compliance and consistency with Gartner Measurement methodologies, comparative databases, and industry experience. Gartner Measurement has examined the assumptions, data, and collection methods and conclusions of Tyco International Ltd. and Kunkle Valve with a view to ensure the cohesion and reasonableness of the findings. In our opinion, the study conforms to REJ methods, and the conclusions drawn by Tyco International Ltd., Kunkle Valve, and Microsoft Corporation are reasonable based on the data provided. This opinion represents the opinion of Gartner Measurement analysts and is not a warranty or representation of any kind with respect to the work performed by Tyco International Ltd., Kunkle Valve, and Microsoft Corporation.

Glossary

24/7 Availability   Functionality that is available 24 hours per day, 7 days per week. In e-commerce terms, the ability for customers and trading partners to interact with suppliers at all times.

Added Value   Additional services or features that differentiate a supplier's goods and services from those of competitors.

Analysis   *See Analytical Systems.*

Analysis Paralysis   The overanalyzing of business and technology requirements, which slows down the development process. Given the fast-moving nature of the Internet, *analysis paralysis* is used to describe the situation in which a solution takes so long to implement that business models and technology have moved on by the time it is rolled out, thereby rendering the solution out of date.

Analytical Systems   Data analysis solutions that are designed to answer strategic business questions. Sometimes referred to as *decision support* systems, *OLAP* (Online Analytical Processing) systems, *business intelligence* systems, or *data warehouses*.

Application   A computer program, usually with a graphical user interface (GUI).

Application Service Provider (ASP)   Companies that host, manage, and administer IT-based solutions, usually for a fee. The solutions are often hosted at the ASP's data centers, rather than the site of the company for which they are run.

Ariba   A business-to-business e-commerce software development company that provides electronic procurement and spending management solutions for Fortune 1000 customers.

Ariba's PunchOut   *See PunchOut.*

ASP   *See Application Service Provider (ASP).*

Authentication   The process of establishing the authenticity of a computer user (or application) by providing credentials such as user names and passwords.

Automated Procurement   *See Electronic Procurement.*

Automation   The replacement of manual actions with computerized operations.

B2B E-Commerce   *See Business-to-Business E-Commerce (B2B E-Commerce).*

B2B Roles   Functions performed by different companies in the B2B e-commerce arena. Example roles include buyer, supplier, Web service provider, market maker, Internet service provider, application service provider, independent software vendor, and so on. Most companies play multiple roles by department such as sales and marketing (supplier) or purchasing (buyer).

B2C E-Commerce   *See Business-to-Consumer E-Commerce (B2C E-Commerce).*

Back-End Integration   The integration of a software solution with existing or new IT applications used internally by a given company such as ERP, CRM, or supply chain.

Bandwidth   A measure of the amount of data that can be passed along a communication channel in a given period of time.

BDM   *See Business Decision Maker (BDM).*

BizTalk Framework   An industry-standard, XML-based framework for reliable document exchange and routing.

BizTalk Mapper   A tool that is part of the Microsoft BizTalk Server 2000 product. BizTalk Mapper allows a developer to define the transformations that must take place to translate one business document format into another.

BizTalk Messaging Manager   A tool that is part of the Microsoft BizTalk Server 2000 product, BizTalk Messaging Manager allows graphical selection of exchange mechanisms and agreements between trading partners.

BizTalk Orchestration Designer   A tool that is part of the Microsoft BizTalk Server 2000 product, BizTalk Orchestration Designer allows a business analyst to model business process interactions visually, and then allows a developer to translate that model into an appropriate solution.

Business Decision Maker (BDM)   Key member of the management team, responsible in part for directing the company's business strategy.

Business Intelligence   *See Analytical Systems.*

Business Models   Generalized strategies that provide the basis for trading. Business models for the Internet Age are currently changing and evolving rapidly.

Business-to-Business E-Commerce (B2B E-Commerce)   The use of the Internet to exchange the data that underpins the buying and selling process between business customers and their suppliers.

Business-to-Consumer E-Commerce (B2C E-Commerce) The use of the Internet to sell goods and services to consumers. Typically, the consumers are members of the general public, although business users can also make purchases from B2C Web sites.

Buy-Side Solutions *See Electronic Procurement.*

Calendaring Services Internet-based services designed to provide shared scheduling between users, companies, or both.

Catalog An itemized collection of product and service information such as part numbers, descriptions, categorization, and pricing. Publishing electronic catalogs online is one of the fundamental concepts in B2B e-commerce.

Certified Partners Large IT solution vendors, such as Microsoft, Oracle, and Sun, operate various programs whereby independent organizations can be certified as meeting standards defined by those vendors. These independent organizations are often known as *certified partners.*

Clarus A B2B e-commerce software development company that provides electronic procurement and electronic marketplace solutions for business customers.

Clarus' Tap-Out *See Tap-Out.*

Collaboration The ability to work with trading partners for mutual benefit. Communicating over the Internet raises new opportunities and challenges for collaboration in the B2B e-commerce arena.

Commerce One A provider of Web-based, electronic marketplace and procurement solutions to Fortune 1000 customers.

Commerce One's RoundTrip *See RoundTrip.*

Commerce Servers Systems that provide the functionality for trading online. Commerce servers typically allow you to design and manage commerce Web sites, manage and publish electronic catalogs, and receive online orders.

Commerce XML (cXML) An industry-standard XML-based e-commerce dialect created by Ariba for defining electronic catalogs, purchase orders, PunchOut, and additional messages.

Commoditization The process whereby one supplier's offering becomes indistinguishable from that of other suppliers.

Commodity An article of trade or commerce which is interchangeable and difficult to differentiate from other products or services of the same type.

Configuration In B2B e-commerce terms, the selection of options that can tailor the product or service being purchased to the needs of the buyer.

Consolidated Payment   An agreement between a company and a financial institution that all payments involved in a particular business process will be settled centrally.

Consultant   A company or individual who provides expert advice. Many organizations provide consulting services to the B2B e-commerce industry.

Critical Success Factors (CSFs)   Influences that affect the realization of a business objective.

CSFs   *See Critical Success Factors (CSFs).*

Customized Solutions   B2B e-commerce solutions that have had their core functionality changed, to some degree, so that they more closely meet specific business needs. Customized solutions are distinct from extended solutions (*see Extended Solutions* for a comparison).

cXML   *See Commerce XML (cXML).*

Database Servers   Software applications that store, manage, and maintain business data.

Differentiation   The ability to distinguish between the goods and services offered by one supplier from those offered by another.

Economic Justification   *See Microsoft REJ.*

EDI   Electronic data interchange (EDI) involves the exchange of business documents between computer systems. Although based on certain standards, EDI implementations are usually proprietary in nature and can be expensive to purchase and maintain.

Electronic Marketplace   An Internet-based network that allows suppliers and buyers to trade electronically.

Electronic Procurement   The automatic processing of information that underpins purchasing procedures. Electronic procurement solutions reduce the amount of human interaction in the purchasing process, and lead to efficiency gains, reduced errors, and other benefits for the buyer.

Electronic Trading   The exchange of business data that underpins the buying and selling process.

E-Mail   An Internet-based system for sending and receiving messages. E-mail messages are usually composed and read by human beings, although some applications can compose, send, and interpret e-mails automatically.

E-Marketplace   *See Electronic Marketplace.*

Empowerment   *See Supplier Empowerment.*

Enterprise Class Solutions   Computer systems and applications that can respond to the heavy demands placed on them by large or high-volume companies.

Enterprise Resource Planning (ERP) Systems   Enterprise resource planning (ERP) systems tie together the processes undertaken by different departments within an organization.

E-Procurement   *See Electronic Procurement.*

ERP Systems   *See Enterprise Resource Planning (ERP) Systems.*

Escrow   An agreement between a grantor, a grantee, and a third party (the escrow agent). The grantor delivers a deed or money to the escrow agent. It is held by the agent until some condition is met, at which time the deed or money is delivered to the grantee. In B2B e-commerce terms, escrow can be provided as a Web service to smooth the business process for suppliers and buyers.

Extended Solutions   B2B e-commerce solutions that have had extra functionality added, to some degree, so that they more closely meet specific business needs. Extended solutions are distinct from customized solutions (*see Customized Solutions* for a comparison).

Extensibility   The ability for a computerized solution to be changed or modified easily by adding features when required.

Extensible Markup Language   *See XML.*

Firewalls   Internet security barriers that protect Web-enabled computer systems from unauthorized access.

Front-End Integration   The integration of an electronic commerce solution with the electronic purchasing, marketplace, or custom applications used by business customers.

Hosted Solutions   IT-based solutions that are managed and administered by a third party, usually for a fee. The solutions are often hosted on the third party's site, rather than the site of the company for which they are run.

HTML   Hypertext Markup Language (HTML) is the industry standard mechanism for displaying text, graphics, and other visual features in a Web browser.

HTTP   Hypertext Transfer Protocol (HTTP) is the industry standard mechanism that allows computers to communicate with each other over the Internet.

Hub-And-Spoke   A model for connecting buyers and suppliers over the Internet, often used with electronic marketplaces. The general idea is that the buyers and suppliers (the "spokes") need to make only one connection to the marketplace or "hub" to be able to trade with many different companies.

Independent Software Vendors (ISVs)   Independent software vendors (ISVs) provide software applications that normally run on a personal computer or server computers. Examples of ISVs used in this book include Microsoft, Ariba, Commerce One, Clarus, SAP, Oracle, and others.

Information Age   A description of the times we are currently living in. The pursuit and exchange of information is involved in many aspects of modern life, especially in the business environment. In fact, information *itself* is now a valuable, often-traded commodity.

Information Revolution   A recent change in business practices in which the role of information has become more important than ever before. The term is often used in comparison to the Industrial Revolution and the Agricultural Revolution of the past.

Integration Servers   Software products that ease the process of allowing one application or solution to communicate with another. Microsoft BizTalk Server is an example of an integration server.

Internet   The infrastructure that connects networks of computers from around the world.

Internet Service Provider (ISP)   Internet service providers (ISPs) supply the physical infrastructure that allows anyone from the largest corporation down to the smallest household to connect to the Internet.

Internet Time   A phrase used to describe the rapidly changing nature of business models and technology. The implication is that *Internet time* proceeds more quickly than *standard* time.

ISP   *See Internet Service Provider (ISP).*

ISVs   *See Independent Software Vendors (ISVs).*

Key Performance Indicators (KPIs)   Key performance indicators (KPIs) are measures of the success or failure of any action or business initiative.

KPIs   *See Key Performance Indicators (KPIs).*

Maintenance, Repair, and Operations (MRO)   Maintenance, repair, and operations costs that almost all businesses incur on a daily basis.

Market Agility   The ability to take on new customers and sales channels and to manage changes quickly and efficiently in response to either evolving market conditions or as part of new, preemptive business strategies.

Market Maker   A type of company that brings suppliers and buyers together. In B2B e-commerce terms, market makers provide message routing, auctions, and other services to facilitate interactions between buyers and suppliers, and usually charge for these facilities.

Marketplace   *See Electronic Marketplace.*

Message Routing   The directing and coordinating of information between computer applications. In B2B e-commerce terms, message routing can involve the direction of business documents such as product information and orders between buyers and suppliers.

Messaging   Although this term can be applied to many different communication mechanisms, it is typically used by IT professionals to describe *asynchronous* communication between computer applications.

Microsoft bCentral   One of Microsoft's solutions for helping small businesses trade online. Microsoft bCentral is a hosted, subscription-based Web service.

Microsoft BizTalk Accelerator for Suppliers   Microsoft's supplier-centric application for allowing suppliers of all sizes to sell more effectively to business customers electronically. The Microsoft BizTalk Accelerator for Suppliers is a core element of the Microsoft Solution for Supplier Enablement.

Microsoft REJ   Microsoft's Rapid Economic Justification framework for analyzing costs, benefits, and return on investments (ROI) in the rapidly changing business and technological environments of modern computing.

MRO   *See Maintenance, Repair, and Operations (MRO).*

MS Market   Microsoft's in-house automated procurement system.

Off-the-Shelf Applications   Solutions that can be bought and installed with a minimal amount of configuration.

Online Auctions   Web services that allow business customers and consumers to bid for products and services.

Online Trading   *See Business-to-Business E-Commerce (B2B E-Commerce).*

Operational Systems   Computer systems that support the day-to-day operation of a business. Data in operational systems is usually volatile in that it can be changed, deleted, or added to in real time.

Out-of-the-Box Applications   *See Off-the-Shelf Applications.*

PC   Personal computer.

Perfect Market   An economist's term for describing certain trading conditions.

Personalization   The ability to present online content to a user that is more relevant to that individual (or his or her company) than standard or generic content.

Pipeline Model   The chaining together of specific actions that are required for an automated business process. Most commonly applied to the processing of orders.

PocketPCs   Hand-held devices with many of the capabilities of standard PCs.

Point-to-Point   A connection mechanism in which one computer or application communicates directly with another in a proprietary manner. Point-to-point connections are often expensive to maintain, especially when compared to connecting over the Internet.

Private Marketplaces   Marketplaces usually run by a large buyer organization for its entire private community of suppliers and other trading partners.

Procurement   The process of purchasing goods and services. *See also Electronic Procurement.*

Publishing   In B2B e-commerce terms, making catalogs or Web services available to trading partners and customers.

PunchOut   Ariba's name for the functionality that delivers *remote shopping* functionality (*see Remote Shopping* for more details).

Rapid Economic Justification   *See Microsoft REJ.*

Rating Services   Web services that allow customers to grade the products and services from different suppliers, thereby aiding the decisions of future purchasers.

Reach   The extent of a supplier's market. B2B e-commerce now allows many suppliers to have *global reach.*

Regional Marketplaces   Marketplaces that are operated to support trade between suppliers and buyers in the same geographical region.

REJ   *See Microsoft REJ.*

Remote Shopping   The process whereby an electronic procurement application or a marketplace browsing session can collaborate with a supplier's sell-side applications and Web site to allow the supplier to expose its own unique value to the purchasing process. It allows suppliers to differentiate their goods and services from those of their competitors so they are not forced to compete on price alone. It also allows suppliers to provide the most up-to-date product information, rather than requiring that buying organizations frequently import the catalogs into their systems.

Risk   The possibility that a certain solution might not deliver the intended benefits to the business.

ROI   Return on investment.

RoundTrip   Commerce One's name for the functionality that delivers *remote shopping* functionality (*see Remote Shopping* for more details).

Sales Channels   Routes through which a supplier can sell goods and services. Some examples include integration with buyers through direct procurement applications, marketplaces, commerce-enabled Web sites, and so on.

Scalability   Used in the IT profession to describe the relationship between increases in computing power and the ability to service more demand. A solution is said to be scalable if an increase in computing power produces a comparable increase in the demand that can be serviced (or a comparable increase in the rate at which a constant demand can be satisfied).

SCM   *See Supply-Chain Management (SCM).*

Sell-Side Solutions   Solutions that enable suppliers to participate and sell electronically to business customers. Typically, sell-side solutions allow the creation, management, and publication of Web sites, electronic catalogs, the receipt and management of business orders, and both front-end and back-end integration capabilities.

Simple Object Access Protocol (SOAP)   A set of rules defining how software functionality is described and accessed over the Internet.

SOAP   *See Simple Object Access Protocol (SOAP).*

Solution Provider   A third party that fulfills outsourced IT requirements, including consulting, application hosting, software applications, and other services.

Solution Vendor   *See Independent Software Vendors (ISVs).*

Subscription-Based Solutions   B2B e-commerce solutions that organizations can use on a subscription basis, most often in hosted scenarios.

Supplier Empowerment   Applied specifically to suppliers in this book, empowerment is the incorporation of B2B e-commerce into selling strategies while allowing suppliers to differentiate themselves and retain control of how their businesses operate.

Supply-Chain Management (SCM)   Supply-chain management (SCM) solutions optimize the flow of products or information so that one step in a business process flows seamlessly into the next.

System Integrators   Third-party consultants and developers with an in-depth, specialized knowledge about implementation of technology solutions.

Tap-Out   Clarus' name for the functionality that delivers remote shopping functionality (*see Remote Shopping* for more details).

Total Cost of Ownership (TCO)   Refers not just to the cost of purchasing a system or solution, but also to the ongoing costs associated with running it. For example, TCO usually includes elements of administrative cost, repair and maintenance costs, and so on.

Trading Partner   Any business customer, supplier, or peer with whom a company builds strategic relationships for the purpose of commerce.

Transaction   In data processing terms, a transaction is a unit of work that must succeed or fail completely. For example, a transaction is often used to refer to one complete purchasing operation or the completed delivery of a business document.

Transformation   The translation of a business document from one electronic form (such as EDI or XML) to another. For example, a solution might define transformations for converting a cXML-based purchase order into a custom format of XML. *See also XSLT.*

UDDI   Universal Description, Discovery, and Integration (UDDI) provides a set of standards that allows companies to expose their business applications (such as order management, procurement, marketing, inventory, and billing systems) as Web services. In addition, UDDI registries function as a type of automated, electronic business white pages. They are Internet-based directories of businesses and the applications that they have exposed for use in B2B e-commerce.

Value Chain Management   Another term for supply-chain management. *See Supply-Chain Management (SCM)* for more details.

W3C   *See World Wide Web Consortium (W3C).*

Web Service Providers   Companies that provide business (and other) services to applications over the Internet. Web service providers are playing an increasingly important role in B2B e-commerce.

Web Services   Software functionality delivered over the Internet.

World Wide Web Consortium (W3C)   Governs the standards used on the Internet, such as HTML, HTTP, XML, and so on.

WSDL   Web Service Description Language (WSDL) describes how software developers can interface with and use Web services.

xCBL   *See XML Common Business Library (xCBL).*

XML   Extensible Markup Language (XML) is the industry standard mechanism for *describing* data. It is a markup language used to structure data so that it can be interpreted by different applications and solutions. It is used extensively to exchange business data between different organizations.

XML Common Business Library (xCBL)   An industry standard XML dialect created and maintained by Commerce One for describing common business documents.

XML Dialects   XML is a standard set of rules for *how* to describe data, but it does not define *what* can be described and what cannot. An XML dialect is a standard set of rules for defining how a particular business document, such as a purchase order or an invoice, is structured. Examples of XML dialects include cXML and xCBL. (*See XML Common Business Library (xCBL)* and *Commerce XML (cXML)* for further details.)

XSLT   Extensible Stylesheet Language for Transformation (XSLT) is a W3C standard that allows a suitably equipped tool or developer to define how a document in one XML dialect can be converted (or transformed) into a different XML dialect. Tools such as Microsoft BizTalk Mapper are based on XSLT.

Index

Learning solutions for *every software user*

Discover how to meet
mission-critical
business needs
with customizable technology solutions!

In today's changing business environment, your success depends on knowing how to stay ahead of the competition. Microsoft and its partners have worked closely with hundreds of business decision-makers to create custom solutions designed to help you get ahead and stay there. These solutions integrate leading technologies, applications, and services into packages tailored to meet mission-critical business needs. A new line of books from Microsoft describes in detail how these solutions can help you speed your time to market and solve your pressing business needs—complete with real-life examples from other businesses.

Get a **Free**
*e-mail newsletter, updates,
special offers, links to related books,
and more when you*

register on line!

Register your Microsoft Press® title on our Web site and you'll get a FREE subscription to our e-mail newsletter, *Microsoft Press Book Connections.* You'll find out about newly released and upcoming books and learning tools, online events, software downloads, special offers and coupons for Microsoft Press customers, and information about major Microsoft® product releases. You can also read useful additional information about all the titles we publish, such as detailed book descriptions, tables of contents and indexes, sample chapters, links to related books and book series, author biographies, and reviews by other customers.

Registration is easy. Just visit this Web page and fill in your information:

http://www.microsoft.com/mspress/register

Microsoft®

Proof of Purchase

Use this page as proof of purchase if participating in a promotion or rebate offer on this title. Proof of purchase must be used in conjunction with other proof(s) of payment such as your dated sales receipt—see offer details.

Supplier Empowerment
0-7356-1498-9

CUSTOMER NAME

Microsoft Press, PO Box 97017, Redmond, WA 98073-9830